Learn

SQL

in a weekend

by **Antonio Padial Solier**

Edition in Spanish: February 2017
Edition in English: October 2020

Design and layout by ©graph*iria*
www.graphiria.com

Table of contents

Preface

Who is this course aimed at?

One of the first decisions that need to be taken into account before elaborating a course like this one is precisely to answer this question: who is this course aimed at? Who is it going to be more useful for?

When talking about the series "Learn in a weekend" the answer is clear: it is aimed at any person who has minimum knowledge on how to use a computer.

With this manual you will not become an expert in the field. I do not intend to deceive anyone. You cannot become an expert overnight, but I can assure you that when you finish this book, you will be able to manage to use SQL in everyday situations.

Are you developing a webpage and you want to use MySQL to store information? Are you studying and you are stuck on the database management subject? Do you want to learn SQL to improve your curriculum or change your career? Or simply, do you have curiosity to learn this language and its possibilities? To all of you, welcome. You have found the appropriate book.

What is the objective?

The key to master any language or software is to have a good base. Spending long hours studying and practising the knowledge is of no use if we do not master its fundamental aspects.

The objective of this book is precisely this one, to help you have a base that is solid and broad enough, not only to be able to use SQL to solve the most common problems, but also to allow you to continue learning in a self-taught way.

The aim, once you finish "Learn SQL in a weekend" is only to depend on yourself to solve complex problems or to learn the most advanced aspects of the language.

How to use it?

All the books of the series "Learn in a weekend" share a series of characteristics.

Firstly, they are eminently practical books. Theory is important, but in computing, the fastest way to learn is practising.

For this reason, it is indispensable to have a computer and to spend the necessary time to create an appropriate environment to conduct tests (do not worry, this is one of the first things you will learn with this course).

Secondly, this course has plenty of examples and exercises with which you can practice what you are learning.

It is very important to complete and understand all of them, but it is also advisable to experiment, trying to solve the problems as you can. There is usually more than one solution for the same problem and you are invited to find them.

And thirdly, the motto "learn in a weekend" is not just a tittle. It is the philosophy of the course. Since time is money, any content that is not important is avoided, to focus on the fundamental aspects of the SQL language.

The course is divided into three blocks that must be fully read and in strict order:

- In the first introductory unit, the first contact takes place and the appropriate environment to practice and do exercises is set.

- A second one where, following the 80-20 rule, we develop the most important concepts, those that are used in most of the cases and that will allow us to solve most of the problems that we will face.

- And finally, a third unit where you will learn more advanced functions and you will develop a little project in which you can put into practice everything you have learnt.

What is the 80-20 rule?

To understand the 80-20 rule or Pareto principle you have to think of the toolbox that you have at home.

How many screwdrivers, screws, pliers, etc. does it contain? For sure, a lot, but now think: how many do you usually use? Typically, in most of the cases (80%), you will only need a Phillips screwdriver, the hammer and maybe some pliers (20% of the tools).

A programming language is just a set of tools that enables us to instruct a computer. In this sense, the Pareto principle establishes that 80% of the problems can be solved with just 20% of the tools.

Obviously, this principle is not exact and does not happen in all cases. However, roughly it is a valid principle.

No matter how versatile and complicated the programming language can be, some elements are always indispensable in most of the cases (20%) while most of the others are only used in some very specific situations (the other 80%).

The objective of the course is to master that 20%, to know the most important things in 80% and to have the necessary base to learn the rest in a self-taught way.

Will I only learn SQL?

No. Although the course is focused on the most important things, it is true that to master it and, above all, to understand what you can do with it, it is advisable to generally learn what a database is, its components, and so on.

For this reason, in this course you will find some parts dedicated to these and some other aspects that are not part of SQL.

Day 1

Welcome to your first day of learning. Today is essential for the success of the course because apart from studying the basic theoretical concepts, you will set your working environment, which is indispensable since without it you will not be able to continue the rest of the days.

Chapter 1.1
Introduction

In this chapter:

> *1. You will learn what a database is and what the role of SQL is when using it.*

What is a database?

A database is a software like an operating system or an antivirus, whose main objective is to store information.

Think of it as a wardrobe with many shelves where you can keep your clothes or as a folder where we keep our notes.

For example, when we log in to Facebook and we post something and submit it, both the text or the photos and videos that we have attached must be stored somewhere to be seen every time we or our contacts access to our profile.

Well, that place is the database and since it is not a person who can understand a natural language but a software, we need a mechanism to indicate it which information to store or what we want to get back. This mechanism is precisely the SQL language

What is the SQL language?

Like any other computer language, SQL *(Structured Query Language)* is just a set of words and a set of rules designed only and exclusively to communicate with a database.

Just like there are several operating systems (Windows, OSX, Linux) and browsers (Chrome, Firefox, Internet Explorer), there are many database management systems (DBMS) like MySQL, Oracle, SQLite, Teradata or SQL Server. Each of them has particular characteristics but with one of them in common, at least: the use of SQL as a communication tool.

What can we do with it?

Basically, we can give three types of instructions to the databases:

- Create and modify its structure. As we will see in future chapters, before storing information, we must create a structure where we can store it. So, we can do it with the SQL language itself.

- Save, modify or delete data.

- And finally, the most used one: we can look for and recover what we have stored thanks to different search criteria.

Chapter 1.2

What is a relational database?

In this chapter:

> *1. You will learn the fundamental elements of the relational model: tables, columns, rows, relations and constraints.*

A bit of theory

Obviously, a database is neither a wardrobe with shelves nor a folder. Its usefulness is the same: storing something in a tidy way so that it will be easy to take it back again. But instead of storing objects, a database is designed to manage information like texts (a name, an email, an address), dates (birthdates, web registry) and numbers mainly.

In this chapter, we have added the word "relational" and it is an important aspect since, although most of databases are relational and in this course we are going to focus on them, there are many other types such as document-oriented, graph, key-value, etc.

The relational model was formulated in the 70s by Edgar Frank Codd and, simplifying a lot, it establishes that a database is formed by the following elements:

- **TABLES:** let's broaden our abstraction and think that a database is a room full of wardrobes. So, each of these is a table.

  That implies that all the information is stored in them therefore they are the fundamental elements of a database.

- **FIELDS OR COLUMNS:** not all the wardrobes (tables) must be the same: some have more shelves, other less but bigger and so on depending on the articles that are going to be stored.

  In a database, these shelves are the columns of the tables. When one is created, apart from naming it, it is necessary to indicate which columns constitute it.

- **ROWS:** simplifying a lot again, a row is the object we store in a specific wardrobe.

  To be stored, it must fit in one of the shelves. It means, we can never store a television in the sugar shelf or the other way around.

  Each row is composed by one or some columns with numbers, texts, etc. that we will store in the database to take them back later.

RELATIONSHIPS: they are the most complex concept to understand and since they are difficult to extrapolate to the real world, the easiest thing is to see them with an example of the relational model.

Let's think of a database where we want to store the list of vehicles that a renting company has. Suppose that for each of them, we want to know the number plate, brand, the cylinder capacity, the combined fuel consumption and the kilometres travelled.

Obviously, the easiest thing is to store everything in a table:

VEHICLES Table

NUMBER PLATE	BRAND	MODEL	CYLINDER CAPACITY	CONSUMPTION	KM
1898 HYT	SEAT	IBIZA 1.4 TDI	1.4	4 l/100 km	23.000
7698 NKK	TOYOTA	VERSO 2.0	2.0	5 l/100 km	12.000
3690 VGB	SEAT	IBIZA 1.4 TDI	1.4	4 l/100 km	125.000
6734 KLM	CITROËN	DS5 2.2	2.2	5 l/100 km	34.000
8965 NMH	TOYOTA	VERSO 2.0	2.0	5 l/100 km	180.000

As you can see, some data from the same model are repeated, like for example what happens with the cylinder capacity and consumption from the SEAT IBIZA 1.4 TDI or the TOYOTA VERSO 2.0.

The relational model enables us to avoid this duplication of information thanks to the use of relations. In the case, the best thing would be to separate the concrete data of the vehicles (number plate, model and km) from the ones that are characteristic of the models (brand, cylinder capacity and consumption).

In other words, on the one hand we would have the following table of vehicles:

VEHICLES Table

NUMBER PLATE	MODEL	KM
1898 HYT	IBIZA 1.4 TDI	23.000
7698 NKK	VERSO 2.0	12.000
3690 VGB	IBIZA 1.4 TDI	125.000
6734 KLM	DS5 2.2	34.000
8965 NMH	VERSO 2.0	180.000

And on the other hand, a table where all the data provided by the manufacturer itself:

VEHICLES Table

MODEL	BRAND	CYLINDER CAPACITY	CONSUMPTION
IBIZA 1.4 TDI	SEAT	1.4	4 l/100 km
VERSO 2.0	TOYOTA	2.0	5 l/100 km
IBIZA 1.4 TDI	SEAT	1.4	4 l/100 km
DS5 2.2	CITROËN	2.2	5 l/100 km
VERSO 2.0	TOYOTA	2.0	5 l/100 km

Both tables would be related by the column "**MODEL**" so if we want to know the general characteristics of a vehicle, it would be enough to turn to the vehicles model table.

To understand the usefulness of this separation, think of a renting company that has 1000 vehicles in its fleet. If the information is not separated, every time a new vehicle is registered, they would need to remember the general characteristics.

By segregating the information, the process of storing the models is much easier since it would be necessary to know neither the cylinder capacity nor the consumption or brand.

● **CONSTRAINTS**: think of a **CONSTRAINT** as a rule that obliges us or bans us to do something when storing data. There are different types of constraints and they are fundamental to be able to store and recover information from our database.

The only and most important one with which we are going to work throughout the course is the one named **PRIMARY KEY** or simply **PK**. Think of this key as the unique name of each of the rows.

Going back to the example of the vehicles:

VEHICLES Table

NUMBER PLATE	MODEL	KM
1898 HYT	IBIZA 1.4 TDI	23.000
7698 NKK	VERSO 2.0	12.000
3690 VGB	IBIZA 1.4 TDI	125.000
6734 KLM	DS5 2.2	34.000
8965 NMH	VERSO 2.0	180.000

What is the column with which we can identify each of the cars of the company without mistakes? For sure, the number plate. It is unique for each car and it does not vary, two of the main three characteristics of a primary key.

The third characteristic is that it cannot be repeated in the same table. It means, there cannot be two rows with the same primary key since we would not be able to identify each of them.

Summarising

You have learnt that in general, a relational database is simply a set of tables that are interrelated.

Each of the tables is made of one or more columns and they are the place where the data is stored such as numbers, dates, texts, images, etc.

Finally, you have learnt that we can establish **CONSTRAINTS** to control the information we store.

Chapter 1.3
Preparing the environment

In this chapter:

> *1. You are going to set everything you need to use SQLite during the rest of the course.*

Why SQLite?

Now that you know what a database is and what SQL is used for, you are ready to configure your test environment.

Throughout the whole course we will use SQLite for the following reasons:

- It does not require installation. As we have said at the beginning, time is money, so we do not want to waste time trying to solve configuration problems.

- It is immensely popular. According to db-engines, (*http://db-engines.com/en/ranking*) in September 2019 SQLite was the eleventh most popular database in the world.

- It is multi-platform so you could use it even if your operating system is Windows, OSX or Linux.

- And, finally, it is free.

Download the software

We do not want you to fill your computer with software that can bother you, so all the applications that we will use are free, do not contain advertisements and in general, they have a "portable" version, which means that they can be used from the hard disc or a USB, without installing anything on your computer.

This guarantees that if at the end of the course you want to leave your computer clean, it would be enough to delete the files.

In the course, we are going to use the software **DB BROWSER FOR SQLITE**, since it is free, light, multi-platform and very easy to use. This software is a graphical interface (GUI: Graphic User Interface) designed to manage and consult SQLite databases.

Browse to *http://sqlitebrowser.org/* and download the version that you need:

- Windows: tagged as PortableApps.

- Mac: tagged as .dmg.

- Linux: .tar.gz.

Once it is downloaded, execute it and you will be ready to continue with the rest of the chapters.

One moment, why do we need a software to use SQLite?

SQLite is a database engine and its role is to store the information and carry out the operations that are sent in the SQL language.

In order to send it these operations, we must use a database manager that is just a software able to communicate with one or more databases. DB Browser for SQLite can only do it with SQLite, but there are others like Toad or DBeaver that can work with other engines Such as MySQL, Oracle, DB2…

Chapter 1.4

What can I store in a database?

In this chapter:

> *1. You will learn the main data types that can be used in SQL.*

> *2. You will understand why it is important to choose the most appropriate one for every situation.*

Why are they necessary?

As we have already commented in the previous chapter, the information of the database lies in tables and each of them is defined by a set of columns. Well, each column can store only one type of data, so choosing the correct ones is indispensable for our database to be used for our purpose, either storing the vehicles from a renting company, the information of a blog or the pictures of our customers.

When we say that a column can only store a single type means that for example, it can only store numbers and we will never be able to store there a text or an image.

And why limiting what we can store in a column? That is to say, why not letting anything in? Simply because not doing so, the databases would be unmanageable.

This does not involve that there aren't products that let this happen. They exist because they are necessary in some cases, but they are products that move outside of the prescribed range of the relational model of Cobb.

The types of data are also important because they make it easier to perform complex operations with the rows of the database. It is very simple to construct a SQL query that totalize the kilometres of our fleet of vehicles. But to do this, the column must be numeric since it is impossible to add the number 100.000, for example, to the text: "The car has 45.000 kilometres".

SQL data types

The most important ones that we will work with throughout the course are:

- **TEXT:** this is the most common one. It is used to store any text such as a name, an ID number or a comment in a blog.

- **NUMBERS:** with or without a decimal place. The difference is important since for a computer it is more difficult to work with the second group.

- **DATES:** this is a type of special data that, apart from storing the date itself, lets us manipulate it by adding or deducting minutes, hours, days...

If you want further information about this topic, in this link from Wikipedia you will find the list of types of SQL (*https://en.wikipedia.org/wiki/SQL#Data_types*), in this one from w3schools you can find the most popular databases (*http://www.w3schools.com/sql/sql_datatypes.asp*) and in this other one, the ones that are admitted by SQLite (*https://www.sqlite.org/datatype3.html*).

One moment, are there different sets of data types?

Computer experts do not like simple things, so, yes, a database can admit types of own data.

SQL is a standard language so it defines the theory, therefore products like SQLite, MySQL or Oracle are the ones that decide how to implement it.

In general, all the databases share 80% of SQL language, but there are always particular characteristics and one of them can be the types of own data, or, what is more common, different names for some of them.

For example, all of them admit integers, although some of them call them **INTEGER** others simply **INT** and there are variations like **BIGINT** or **SMALLINT**. It is also usual to find the type of text (**TEXT**) and other derivatives such as **CLOB**, one special that admits up to 4 GB of information in just a column.

This implies that when you start working with a product that is not SQLite, one of the first things that you will need to check is the data that it admits.

SQLite

The four types that we will work with throughout the course are:

- **INTEGER**: it lets store an integer, either positive or negative.

- **TEXT**: to store text.

- **REAL**: numbers, either positives or negatives, but with decimal places.

- **DATETIME**: dates.

Another particular characteristic of SQLite is that it does not allow us to limit the size of a field. In other databases like Oracle or MySQL when you define a numeric field or text field, we specify also its maximum size. That is to say, when we say that a column will store Spanish postcodes, we can limit it up to five characters that is the maximum they can have.

It is an important mechanism to control that the information stored is correct and to facilitate the job of the database when storing and recovering the information. However, it is not indispensable to fulfil our objective to learn how to use SQL.

In any case and although it does not follow the constraint, SQLite enables us to indicate the maximum size when creating our columns, so we will do it like that throughout the course.

Chapter 1.5
Your first database

In this chapter:

> *1. You will learn the basics of the software **DB BROWSER FOR SQLITE**.*
>
> *2. You will create your first database.*

Creating a database

Well, you already know what a database is and what we can store in it, apart from knowing what SQL is and what it is used for. So, now you only need to open **DB BROWSER FOR SQLITE** and create one.

Execute the software and select the menu option File > New Database. A browser will appear for you to give it a name and select where to save it (in SQLite the database will be saved as just one file). I have chosen **"MYSHOP"**. Assign the extension .sqlite3 because it will make your job easier when opening it again.

Then, an assistant with the title "Edit table definicion" will appear. It allows us to create tables with the visual editor. Click on "Cancel", since the idea is to make everything with SQL directly.

And finally, the complete interface of the software will appear with the database **MYSHOP** opened. Yes, you have already created your first database!

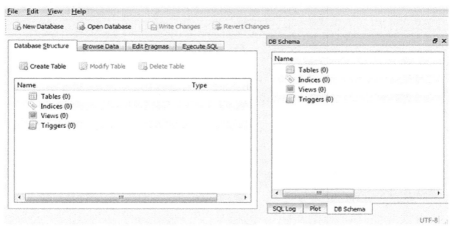

Main window..

The options that we will use the most throughout the course are:

- **Toolbar:** we will use it to save the changes we will do on our databases ("Write Changes") apart from creating and opening the database.

- In the tab "Database Structure" from the main section we will be able to see a summary of the objects of our database: some known as the tables and others that you will learn throughout the course like indexes or views.

- The tab "Browse Data" will let us see at a glance the content of a table or a view.

- "Execute SQL" is the tab that we will use the most since it is where we will write and execute our SQL queries.

- The tab "SQL Log" in the right section will also be very useful since you will be able to see the queries that are being executed against the database (by ourselves or **DB BROWSER FOR SQLITE**).

Is a database just a file?

In SQLite, yes. A database is just a simple file were all the tables, columns, rows, etc. are stored.

But this does not mean that in all the products it is like this. In fact, a database is usually managed through a lot of files and directories. This depends on the product and the size of the database since it is not the same to manage the entries of a blog than the transactions of a bank entity.

Chapter 1.6
Creating tables

In this chapter:

> *1. You will create tables with different columns and types.*
>
> *2. You will write your first SQL queries.*
>
> *3. You will use the abilities that are provided by **DB BROWSER FOR SQLITE** to explore the tables of a database.*
>
> *4. You will learn the meaning of the concepts "schema" and "instance".*

A small act of faith

Although it is true that in the introduction we suggested that to master a language the best thing is to understand and experiment with each and every example, for the rest of the first day we ask you to have an act of faith and execute the queries as they are written without stopping to think what they mean.

The idea is that first you get a complete view of the fundamental operations (creating a database, creating a table, inserting rows and consulting data) and then you continue to delve into all of them in the second day of the course.

Your first table and therefore, your first SQL query

As we have commented in the previous chapter, the software allows us to create and edit tables thanks to a visual menu (options "Create Table" and "Modify Table" from the tab "Database Structure") but the best thing is to learn how to do it with SQL queries.

We are going to create one with the name **"USERS"** that will store the information of the users of our web. At the moment, it will have three columns: **ALIAS** that will be the user name; **EMAIL** where we will keep the email addresses and **PASSWORD** where we will keep the passwords.

Open the tab "Execute SQL" and write the following:

```
CREATE TABLE USERS (
ALIAS TEXT,
EMAIL TEXT,
PASSWORD TEXT)
```

We will delve into the structure of the SQL queries later one, but what concerns to this one:

- CREATE TABLE is the SQL query (the "magic word") that is used to create tables..

- Later, and in between brackets there are the columns of the table itself. They are defined with a name and the type of data, that in this case is TEXT in the three cases.

Now we have to execute the query. To do this, click on the icon "PLAY" and if everything has gone well, the following will appear in the text box from below:

Query executed successfully: CREATE TABLE USERS (
ALIAS TEXT,
EMAIL TEXT,
PASSWORD TEXT) (took 1ms)

Now change to the tab "Database Structure" and you will be able to check that in the section "Tables" the table **USERS** that we have just created has appeared.

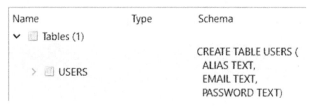

Structure of the table USERS.

Finally, we will save the changes that we have made to the database. To do this, press on the option "Write Changes" from the toolbar. This is a peculiarity from SQLite and you must take it into account throughout the course: every time that you perform an operation and you want to save it you must press this option.

We will delve into this later on, but it is necessary to highlight that in other databases the operation of creating or deleting a table is irreversible, which means, there is not a "Write Changes" o a "Revert Changes".

Schema and Instance

Until now the only thing that we have created is a database with an empty table, it means, a "container" of information. Well, this container, that is to say, the set of elements which constitute a database except for the data itself, it is usually referred to as "database schema".

As for the "database instance" is a database with content.

Making a comparison with the real world, think of a wardrobe manufacturer who designs a new model, or what is the same, he or she designs a new "database schema". Later, he or she manufactures 1000 units and they are sold to different customers. Well, each of these thousand wardrobes would be a "database instance".

The normal thing is that a database is created based on a schema to provide service to some type of software like WordPress.

This is one of the most used platforms to create blogs and its functioning is based on a MySQL database that is where all the articles, comments, etc. are stored.

Well, when we install WordPress one of the first things that need to be done is creating a new MySQL database instance from a predefined schema.

This instance is the one that the blog uses to store information, which means, all the blogs done with WordPress share a "database schema" (they have a database with the same number of tables, columns, indexes and relations).

Chapter 1.7

Store and query data

In this chapter:

> *1. You will learn how to save rows in a table using SQL queries.*
>
> *2. You will use **DB BROWSER FOR SQLITE** to see the content of the tables.*
>
> *3. You will create your first SQL queries to check data.*

Insert records in a table

You can save rows through the visual interface (button "New Record" from the tab "Browse Data") or as we will do it throughout the course: through the query INSERT INTO.

Delete the content of the tab "Execute SQL" and write the following:

```
INSERT INTO USERS
VALUES ('admin','admin@myshop.com','pa$$w0rd')
```

- ● INSERT INTO: it shows that we want to save rows in a table.

- ● VALUES: it is used to establish the values of each of the columns. These are specified between brackets and separated by commas (,). In general, the texts are delimited between single quotes ('). This is common to almost all the programming languages.

Now execute and, if everything went well, you will see the following message:

Query executed successfully: INSERT INTO USERS VALUES ('admin','admin@myshop.com','pa$$w0rd') (took 0ms)

We have just stored the data of the user *"admin"* whose e-mail is *"admin@myshop.com"* and his password *"pa$$w0rd"*.

Now we are going to create a new one:

INSERT INTO **USERS**
VALUES *('guest','guest@yahoo.es','pwd')*

Query executed successfully: INSERT INTO USERS VALUES
('guest','guest@yahoo.es','pwd') (took 0ms)

Obviously, SQL provides us with tools to insert several rows at the same time, but this is something we will learn in later chapters.

Very well, now that you have created two rows, we only need to see them to check that everything went well.

Show the content of a table

To check that the information has been correctly saved we can use the tab "Browse Data". This is a very useful option and that you will use a lot since many times it is more comfortable to see the content of a table directly here than constructing SQL queries.

Content of the table USERS.

🦐 In the top left list, we can select any table of the database to see its information.

🦐 Independently from the number of rows of the table, the browser will only show us a few of them directly. If we want to see more, we can use the controls below to go through it little by little, to go to the beginning or end and so on.

🦐 The boxes called "Filter" search for rows as if they were a spreadsheet.

Query data

SELECT lets us query for data in a table. This is one of the main functions of SQL so it is one of the words that you will use the most throughout the course.

Write and execute the following query (remember, query is the name we give to a SQL command):

```
SELECT * FROM USERS
WHERE ALIAS = 'admin'
```

If everything went well you will see a grid with an only row and a confirmation message below:

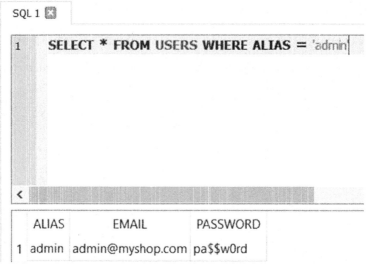

SQL executed with its result..

SQL is a language designed to be natural so, as when creating tables (CREATE TABLE) and when storing rows (INSERT INTO), the syntax to retrieve data is quite understandable.

We start with the keyword SELECT that orders the database to look for information. Later, we name the columns to show. If we need all of them, we can use the asterisk symbol (*).

Then, we must indicate which tables to look for, so we use the word FROM with the name of the table.

Finally, we tell the database which rows we want to get back: all of them or the ones that meet some conditions. For this, we will use WHERE and in this case, the condition that specifies that we are looking for those whose ALIAS is "admin".

To sum up, what we have asked the database is: "Show me the alias, the email and the password of the users whose alias is 'admin'".

Eventually, it is important to highlight that we usually talk about looking for or consulting information, which means, after inserting rows in the database, we ask it some questions.

This implies that contrary to the comparison with the wardrobe where we store and take out objects, the reading of information in a database is not destructive, it means, the information is still there until we delete it explicitly.

What can we ask to a database?

Well, practically anything. Despite its simplicity, SQL is a very versatile language that is fostered by the own characteristics of each product.

Depending on how we ask the question and the information that is stored in the database, we will obtain different types of answers. This is something we will delve into the second day but for you to start having an idea you can try executing the following queries:

All the users whose **ALIAS** is not 'admin':

```
SELECT * FROM USERS
WHERE ALIAS ! = 'admin'
```

Total number of users registered:

```
SELECT COUNT (1) FROM USERS
```

Users whose **ALIAS** is 'anonymous':

```
SELECT * FROM USERS
WHERE ALIAS = 'anonymous'
```

Chapter 1.8

First day summary

In brief

Congratulations! You have finished the first day of the course and therefore, you already have the basic knowledge to continue with your learning process of SQL language.

Throughout this day you have learnt that a database is simply a software designed to store information in many forms like texts, dates, images, numbers, etc. and that SQL is the standard language that is used to manipulate it and to retrieve data.

You have also learnt what the term "relational" really means and which elements form a database: tables, columns, rows relationships and constraints, mainly.

As with any type of software, there are many products in the market, each of them with their own characteristics and therefore, more or less appropriate depending on what they are going to be used for. It is not the same to save the content of a blog than the call history of a mobile network operator.

In this course, we have chosen SQLite since it is free, strong and easy to install. You have configured the tool **DB BROWSER FOR SQLITE** that is free, multiplatform, has all the basic functions and is easy to use as the database.

And, finally you have made your first operations on a database: create it, create a table, insert rows and retrieve data.

Day 2

In contrast with the first day where the chapter was more theoretical, the ones that are awaiting you now are mostly practical. You will write a lot of SQL queries, so try all of them as we previously commented, experiment and put into practice what you are learning.

Chapter 2.1

SQL language

In this chapter:

> *1. You will learn the general characteristics of the SQL language.*
>
> *2. The rules for naming the tables, columns, etc. of a database are enumerated.*
>
> *3. We will review the different data types that exists.*

Introduction

SQL was born in the 70's at the research IBM labs. It was designed thanks to the works of E.F. Codd (inventor, as we commented before, of the relational model) to be able to manage and make queries against the database.

It is not a programming language like PHP or Java, but as its acronym shows *(Structured Query Language)* it is a language to make queries, in this case, against a database. This implies that it is more limited, easy and therefore, easier to learn.

As well as with a "real" language, SQL is formed by a series of keywords (the lexicon) that can be combined following some rules (the grammar). In the next chapters, you will delve into the use of the most important ones, either alone or in combination with others to generate more complex queries.

Keywords

They are the fundamental elements of the language since they indicate the database what it has to do: create a table, insert data, search for some type of information, etc. as we said before, they are the "magic words".

Some examples are INSERT, TEXT o SELECT. Although in the book you are going to see them always written in capital letters, it does not matter the way you write them, SQLite will recognise them anyway.

These words are reserved to give instructions to the database so you cannot use them as names for the tables, columns, etc. To check this, execute this query in SQLite:

```
CREATE TABLE SELECT (COLUMN TEXT)
```

Names

This is the way we call an object in the database. All of them must have a name and this must be unique among its class. This implies that there cannot be two tables with the same name as well as two equal columns inside the same table.

On the other hand, as it happens with the keywords, it does not matter whether you write the names in capital letters or lower case, because for SQLite all the letter are capital letters.

For example, if you create a table called "**User**", later you will not be able to create a table called "**USER**":

To check this, first execute this query:

```
CREATE TABLE User
(NAME TEXT)
```

Later, the following query. If everything went well, an error will occur.

```
CREATE TABLE USER
(NAME TEXT)
```

All the names must begin with a letter and they cannot contain some special symbol, spaces or arithmetic operators like the addition one (+) or multiplication (*). For instance, the following names would be correct:

- **USERS1**: starts with a letter.

- **_USERS**: the low bar is not a forbidden symbol.

Whereas the following ones are incorrect:

- **1USERS**: it starts with a number.

- **USERS OF MY WEB**: it contains spaces.

- **US*ERS**: it has a forbidden operator (*)

These constraints are aimed at avoiding misunderstandings when interpreting a SQL query. For example, if the use of words reserved as names of tables was permitted, SQLite would not be able to know if the following query was correct or we have just simply committed a mistake when writing it.

```
INSERT INTO INTO
VALUES (1,2,3)
```

Does the user want to insert a row into the table "INTO" or he has made a mistake writing the query and repeated the keyword?

Operators

The third distinctive element of SQL is the operators. These, let us make calculations (adding, subtracting, dividing…), logical and comparison operations (bigger than, smaller than…) among columns, rows, etc.

Try executing the following:

```
SELECT 1 + 2 FROM USERS
```

You will see that instead of giving back the content of the columns from the table **USERS**, the database "answers" with the result of adding 1 and 2, which is what we have asked for with the expression "1+2".

Data Types

The last elements that compose the language are the types of data, which are the different types of values that we can save in the columns of a table. As we advanced in the first chapters of the book, the ones that we will use in the course are:

- **INTEGER**: it allows us to store a whole number, either positive or negative.

- **TEXT**: to store text.

- **REAL**: positives or negatives decimal numbers.

- **DATETIME**: dates.

Spaces and line separators

Although it is advisable to be as clear and organised as possible when writing queries, SQL is very flexible in this sense and lets us use spaces, line breaks and tabulations.

In order to check it, try executing the following queries as they are written:

All in just one line:

```
SELECT * FROM USERS
```

With line breaks:

```
SELECT
*
FROM USERS
```

With line breaks and tabulations:

```
SELECT *
    FROM USERS
```

As long as there is a space between the keyword and the names, SQLite will be able to recognise the instructions we are giving it.

Finally, it is important to highlight that it is not necessary to execute the queries one by one. We can write several and execute them sequentially. To do this, you must separate them with the character (;).

For example:

```
CREATE TABLE CARS (NUMBERPLATE TEXT);
INSERT INTO CARS VALUES ('4765 AFG');
SELECT * FROM CARS;
DROP TABLE CARS;
```

- Firstly, we create the table **CARS** with just one column **NUMBERPLATE**.

- We insert a value.

- We show the content of the table.

- And to finish, we delete it with DROP TABLE.

When finishing the execution, you will see in the result area the row with the number plate "4765 AFG" and in the log, the result of the last instruction:

Query executed successfully: DROP TABLE CARS; (took 0ms)

Try executing again the query SELECT. You can do this by deleting the other three or selecting the text that you want to execute and click on the corresponding icon.

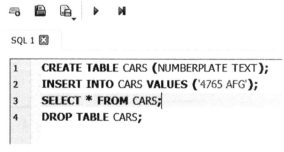

We highlight a line to execute it alone.

The error message indicates that the table "CARS" does not exist because you previously deleted it.

no such table: CARS: SELECT * FROM CARS;

Chapter 2.2

Create, Alter and Drop Table

In this chapter:

> *1. You will learn to create and modify tables.*
>
> *2. You will use the query DROP TABLE to delete them.*
>
> *3. You will learn to define columns with a predetermined length.*

CREATE TABLE

The first thing we must do to use a database is to create the tables that are going to form it through the statement CREATE TABLE whose syntax is:

 **¡IMPORTANT!**

CREATE TABLE **table_name** (
column_name_1 COLUMN_TYPE_1 *(column_size_1)*,
column_name_2 COLUMN_TYPE_2 *(column_size_2)*,
column_name_3 COLUMN_TYPE_3 *(column_size_3)*
)

- CREATE TABLE: keywords that indicate that what we are going to do is defining a table.

- **table_name**: later, we assign it a name. Remember the constraints that you learnt in the previous chapter.

- **column_name** COLUMN_TYPE *(column_size)*: Finally, we enumerate the columns separated by commas with the name, type and, optionally, the size of each of them.

As an example, we are going to create one with the data of each type and different lengths.

With the following query we have created the table **TYPES_TEST** with five columns: **SHORT_TEXT, LONG_TEXT, NUMERIC_DATE, DATE AND DECIMAL_NUMBER**.

```
CREATE TABLE TYPES_TEST (
SHOT_TEXT TEXT (5),
LONG_TEXT TEXT (500),
NUMERIC_DATE INTEGER (8),
DATE DATETIME,
DECIMAL_NUMBER REAL (8,3)
)
```

Defining the size of the columns

As we have seen in the example, the size is specified with a number between brackets next to the name of the column itself.

This constraint cannot be applied to the data type **DATETIME**. In the rest of the cases, the size means the following:

- **INTEGER**: it limits the maximum number of digits in a number. So, an INTEGER column of size 4 can store values from -9999 to 9999.

- **TEXT**: similar to the previous case, the size indicates the maximum number of letters (including spaces) that a text can have. For instance, one of 4 positions cannot store the name "Roberto".

- **REAL**: in this case, the length is expressed with two digits. The first of them is the total number of digits and the second the number of digits for the decimal place. So, a REAL of 9,2 size can store from -9999999.99 to 9999999.99 (7 + 2 decimal places = 9 digits in total).

• •

 EXERCISES

To practice, try to work out if the following values are correct depending on the column they are trying to be saved:

    1. **COST** column of REAL *(6,2)* type
        a) -1814
        b) 2015,23
        c) -1456,567
        d) 23
        e) 12,887

                        SOLUTION: YES: a), b) and d) / NO: c) and e)

    2. **OBJECT** column of TEXT *(10)* type
        a) Light bulb
        b) Low-energy bulb
        c) Glass
        d) Tall glass

                      SOLUTION: YES: a), c) and d) / NO: b)

• • • • • • • • • • • • • • • • • • •

Before learning to modify a table, we are going to practice a little bit with the instruction CREATE TABLE *with the next exercise:*

*Create the table "*CUSTOMER*" with the columns and types that are necessary to store the following information:*

- Name: consider a maximum number of 40 characters.
- Surname: 100 characters, maximum.
- ID: decide which type and size are the most appropriate.
- Address: 300 characters, maximum.
- Membership number: we think that our shop can get to have 9.999 customers.
- Date of birth: use the DATETIME type.
- Age: think of which must be the best type and the appropriate length.
- Points: the shop will let the customers have a maximum of 99999 points. The points can have 2 places after the decimal point..

An example of a valid table would be:

```
CREATE TABLE CUSTOMER (
NAME TEXT (40),
SURNAME TEXT (100),
ID TEXT (9),
ADRESS TEXT (300),
MEMBER_NUM INTEGER (4),
BIRTH_DATE DATETIME,
AGE INTEGER (3),
POINTS REAL (7,2),
)
```

To take into account:

- In Spain, an ID can contain 8 numbers and a control char, so the minimum type is TEXT (9).

- The membership number must be an INTEGER (4) and the age an INTEGER (3) since the customers will always be younger than 999 years old.

- The points need 5 digits before decimal point and two after it, so that is why the key is a REAL (7,2).

ALTER TABLE

Although the normal thing is to have the name and what we want to store in the table really clear when we create it, in some time maybe we need to store something else, modify its name or delete columns.

Think, for example, of the table CUSTOMER from the previous exercise. What if we need to store the telephone number of the customers? Or, what can we do if we want to change its name to **CUSTOMERS** because it is clearer? Could we delete the column **AGE** if we do not consider it important anymore?

To solve these situations, we will use the instruction ALTER TABLE that has the following variants:

● **ALTER TABLE – RENAME TO**: this lets us modify the name of one table from the database:

 **¡IMPORTANT!**

ALTER TABLE table_name
RENAME TO new_table_name

For example:

ALTER TABLE **CUSTOMER**
RENAME TO **CUSTOMERS**

● **ALTER TABLE – ADD COLUMN**: as you can imagine, this lets us add columns to our tables.

 **¡IMPORTANT!**

ALTER TABLE table_name
ADD COLUMN column_name column_type *(column_size)*

To add the telephone number to **CUSTOMERS**, we just have to execute:

ALTER TABLE **CUSTOMERS**
ADD COLUMN **TEL_NUMBER** INTEGER *(9)*

● **ALTER TABLE – DROP COLUMN**: if we do not need any of our columns anymore, we can delete it with this instruction:

For example, to delete the column **AGE**, we must execute:

> ALTER TABLE **CUSTOMERS**
> DROP COLUMN **AGE**

The output is:

> *near: "DROP": syntax error:*

No, you did not make any mistake when writing the query. When executing it, you will see an error. This is because, like any other database, SQLite has its characteristics and limitations and this is one of the most remarkable ones: **we cannot delete columns from a table that we have already createds.**

● **ALTER TABLE – RENAME COLUMN**: finally, with this variant, you will be able to change the name of the columns.

Just like the previous query, this one is not permitted in SQLite but it is important for you to know it. An example would be:

> ALTER TABLE **CUSTOMERS**
> RENAME COLUMN **NUM_POINTS** TO **POINTS**

 **EXERCISES**

Write the SQL queries needed to make the following changes in the table **CUSTOMERS***:*

- Add a column to register **EMAIL** addresses of up to 50 characters long.
- Add another one for the **LANDLINE** phones.
- Delete the column for **POINTS** since this special offer has already finished.
- Replace **ID** with **TAX ID NUMBER** so you can also register freelances as customers of the shop.

The solution would be (consider that the last two do not work in SQLite because of the limitations we commented before):

```
ALTER TABLE CUSTOMERS
ADD COLUMN EMAIL TEXT (50);

ALTER TABLE CUSTOMERS
ADD COLUMN NUM_TEL_LANDLINE INTEGER (9);

ALTER TABLE CUSTOMERS
DROP COLUMN POINTS;

ALTER TABLE CUSTOMERS
RENAME COLUMN DNI TO TAX_ID_NUMBER;
```

DROP TABLE

This is the last instruction that you will learn in this chapter. It is used to delete tables so it is quite dangerous since when you delete a table, all the data will be lost:

 **¡IMPORTANT!**

```
DROP TABLE table_name
```

To practice we are going to clean a little bit our database:

```
DROP TABLE TYPES_TEST;
DROP TABLE USERS;
DROP TABLE USER;
```

Chapter 2.3

Insert into

In this chapter:

1. You will learn to insert rows into a table.

INSERT INTO

Well, you have already learnt how to create, modify and delete tables, so you would be wondering: How can I fill them with content? I mean, how can I store information in them? Very simple, Thanks to the query INSERT INTO:

> ### ¡IMPORTANT!
>
> INSERT INTO **table_name**
> VALUES *(value_1, value_n)*
>
> - INSERT INTO: this is the query that indicates to the database that we want to insert a new row in our table.
>
> - **nombre_tabla**: name of the table where we are going to store data.
>
> - VALUES: list of the values to save.
>
> - *(valor_1, valor_n)*: values to assign in each of the columns of the table "**table_name**" separated by commas (,).

As always, the best way to understand it by practising. If you have executed all the queries up to now, you will have a table called **CUSTOMERS** with the following columns in your database:

NAME, SURNAME, ID, ADDRESS, MEMBER_NUM BIRTH_DATE, AGE, POINTS, TEL_NUMBER, EMAIL, NUM_TEL_LANDLINE.

We are going to create a new row executing:

```
INSERT INTO CUSTOMERS
VALUES (
'ROBERTO','SUÁREZ GIL','78665424D',
'CALLE MAYOR Nº5',1,'1978-08-21',
32,12.45,679867456,
NULL, 913479567)
```

To take into account:

- The values that we are going to save in the columns of TEXT type are delimited by simple quotes ('). The need to use separators in texts is common among all programming languages.

- Numbers do not need any type of delimitation.

- To specify decimal places, we will use a point (.).

- The dates must be written following the following format: year (4 digits) – month (2 digits) – day (2 digits), for example '1978-08-21'.

- NULL is the word reserved by SQL to represent a null value, which means, that in this column no value will be saved.

Now, if we go to the tab "Browse Data" we will see the content of the table with the row we have just inserted:

Database Structure   Browse Data   Edit Pragmas   Execute SQL

Table: CUSTOMERS

NAME	SURNAME	ID	ADDRESS	MEMBER_NUM
Filter	Filter	Filter	Filter	Filter
1 ROBERTO	SUÁREZ GIL	78665424D	CALLE MAY...	1

First row of the table.

In this case, we have specified a value for each of the columns, although it is not necessary. This means SQL lets us omit columns when we create a new row. To do this, we use a variant of the query INSERT INTO:

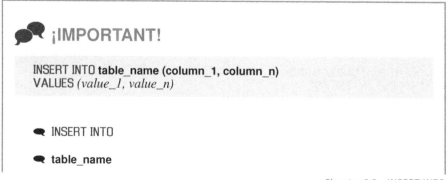

¡IMPORTANT!

INSERT INTO table_name (column_1, column_n)
VALUES (value_1, value_n)

- INSERT INTO

- table_name

- **(column_1, column_n)**: names of the columns separated by commas.
- **VALUES**
- *(value_1, value_n)*: values to save in each one.

We are going to insert a new row storing only the name and surnames:

```
INSERT INTO CUSTOMERS (NAME, SURNAME)
VALUES ('ANTONIO', 'SÁNCHEZ CABALLERO')
```

By default, the database will assign the value NULL to the fields in which we have not saved a value.

	NAME	SURNAME	ID	ADDRESS	MEMBER_NUN	BII
	Filter	Filter	Filter	Filter	Filter	Filt
1	ROBERTO	SUÁREZ GIL	78665424D	CALLE MAY...	1	197
2	ANTONIO	SÁNCHEZ C...	NULL	NULL	NULL	NU.

In the second row there are columns without value.

By specifying the columns, we are also determining the order in which they will appear in the list VALUES. For example, to insert the previous row, we could have also executed:

```
INSERT INTO CUSTOMERS (SURNAME, NAME)
VALUES ('SÁNCHEZ CABALLERO', 'ANTONIO')
```

On the contrary, if we do not include the list of columns in the query, SQLite will expect to find values for each of them. If there is one missing, an error will occur.

Try to execute the following:

```
INSERT INTO CUSTOMERS
VALUES ('ROBERTO')
```

table CUSTOMERS has 11 columns but 1 values were supplied:
INSERT INTO CUSTOMERS VALUES ('ROBERTO')

 **EXERCISES**

Create INSERT INTO *sentences to store the following customers:*

- HÉCTOR GARCÍA PASCUAL, with a membership number 123, born on 3rd of May 1979, and landline telephone 916897654.
- SILVIA ROMERO FERNÁNDEZ, with ID number 78665432Q who lives in 23 Manuela Malasaña Street in Madrid.
- LAURA MARÍN SÁNCHEZ, 45 years old, 345.67 points and email address lmarsanchez@tucorreo.es.
- ANTONIO SÁNCHEZ CABALLERO, born on Jun 5, 1968.

The solution could be:

INSERT INTO **CUSTOMERS (NAME, SURNAME, MEMBER_NUM, BIRTH_ DATE, NUM_TEL_LANDLINE)**
VALUES *('HÉCTOR', 'GARCÍA PASCUAL', 123, '1979-05-03', 916897654);*

INSERT INTO **CUSTOMERS (NAME, SURNAME, ID, ADDRESS)**
VALUES *('SILVIA', 'ROMERO FERNÁNDEZ', '78665432Q', 'Calle Manuela Malasaña 23. Madrid');*

INSERT INTO **CUSTOMERS (NAME, SURNAME, AGE, POINTS, EMAIL)**
VALUES *('LAURA', 'MARÍN SÁNCHEZ', 45, 345.67, 'lmarsanchez@ tucorreo.es');*

INSERT INTO **CUSTOMERS (NAME, SURNAME, BIRTH_DATE)**
VALUES *('ANTONIO', 'SÁNCHEZ CABALLERO', '1968-06-05');*

If everything went well, we will see the following in the tab "Browse Data":

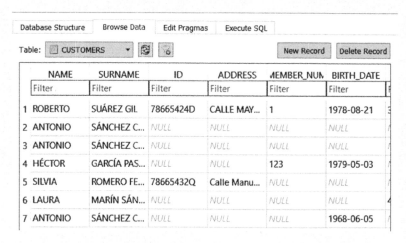

	NAME	SURNAME	ID	ADDRESS	MEMBER_NUN	BIRTH_DATE	
	Filter	Filter	Filter	Filter	Filter	Filter	
1	ROBERTO	SUÁREZ GIL	78665424D	CALLE MAY...	1	1978-08-21	3
2	ANTONIO	SÁNCHEZ C...	NULL	NULL	NULL	NULL	
3	ANTONIO	SÁNCHEZ C...	NULL	NULL	NULL	NULL	
4	HÉCTOR	GARCÍA PAS...	NULL	NULL	123	1979-05-03	
5	SILVIA	ROMERO FE...	78665432Q	Calle Manu...	NULL	NULL	
6	LAURA	MARÍN SÁN...	NULL	NULL	NULL	NULL	4
7	ANTONIO	SÁNCHEZ C...	NULL	NULL	NULL	1968-06-05	

List of customers.

One moment, can there be three customers with the name ANTONIO SÁNCHEZ CABALLERO? Absolutely, since in a table, unless we do something to control it, there are no constraints over the limits of the types of data when inserting rows. This is why we were able to create two rows in which the same person appears.

The normal thing is that we want to control that there are not two customers with the same full name, or two cars with the same number plate in the database of a renting company, etc. To do this, we will use constraints (CONSTRAINTS), issue that we will delve into in the next chapter.

• •

Chapter 2.4

Usage of Primary Key

In this chapter:

> *1. We will study what the constraints of a relational database are.*
>
> *2. You will learn to establish the so-called PRIMARY KEY CONSTRAINT, essential for almost all the tables.*

What are the constraints?

A constraint is just a prohibition, a rule to be followed by each row of a table. There are constraints of different types, but the essential and with the one we will be working throughout the course is PRIMARY KEY or just PK.

This establishes that there cannot be two rows with the same values in a set of columns. For example, if we are storing customers on a table, we can define the PK in the **ID** column, avoiding this way that there are two people with the same ID.

With a few exceptions, all the tables in a relational database have PK.

Going back to the example we saw the first day about a table with models of vehicles:

MODEL	BRAND	CYLINDER_CAPACITY	CONSUMPTION
IBIZA 1.4 TDI	SEAT	1.4	4 l/100 km
VERSO 2.0	TOYOTA	2.0	5 l/100 km
DS5 2.2	CITROËN	2.2	5 l/100 km

In this case, the PK could be formed just by the column **MODEL** since it is not very probable that two brand names share the same name for the models. If we are not sure about this, we can establish a PK with two columns: **BRAND** and **MODEL**, making sure that they will never be repeated this way.

We can define the PK when we create a table or later. Let's see how:

- **PRIMARY KEY in the creation of a table: Only one column:** if we want that only one column forms the PK of a table, we just need to add the reserved word PRIMARY KEY after its type in the CREATE TABLE sentence.

For example:

```
CREATE TABLE MODELS (
BRAND TEXT (30),
MODEL TEXT (100) PRIMARY KEY,
CYLINDER_CAPACITY TEXT (10),
CONSUMPTION (15))
```

If everything went well, we will see the following table in the tab "Database Structure".

		CREATE TABLE MODELS (BRAND TEXT (30), MODEL TEXT (100) PRIMARY KEY, CYLINDER_CAPACITY TEXT (10), CONSUMPTION TEXT (15))
⌄ ☐ MODELS		
☐ BRAND	TEXT(30)	`BRAND` TEXT(30)
☐ MODEL	TEXT(100)	`MODEL` TEXT(100)
☐ CYLINDER_CAPACITY	TEXT(10)	`CYLINDER_CAPACITY` TEXT(10)
☐ CONSUMPTION	TEXT(15)	`CONSUMPTION` TEXT(15)

The key icon in a column shows that it is part of the PK.

Now we are going to insert a row in the table **MODELS**:

```
INSERT INTO MODELS (BRAND, MODEL)
VALUES ('SEAT', 'IBIZA 1.4 TDI')
```

Query executed successfully: INSERT INTO MODELS (BRAND, MODEL) VALUES ('SEAT', 'IBIZA 1.4 TDI') (took 1ms)

As it is the first row, it cannot be repeated so it is correctly saved in the table.

Now, we are going to try with the following query:

```
INSERT INTO MODELS (BRAND, MODEL)
VALUES ('RENAULT', 'IBIZA 1.4 TDI')
```

UNIQUE constraint failed: MODELS.MODEL: INSERT INTO MODELS (BRAND, MODEL) VALUES ('RENAULT', 'IBIZA 1.4 TDI')

The database returns an error since if this value were saved, there would be two rows with the same value in the column **MODEL** that is the PK of the table.

● **PRIMARY KEY in the creation of the table. Several columns:** Another possibility is that the PK is formed by two or more columns. In this case, we will also use the word **PRIMARY KEY**, but this time, before the set of columns that will form it.

> 💬 **¡IMPORTANT!**
>
> ```
> CREATE TABLE table_name (
> column_name_1 column_type_1 (column_size_1),
> column_name_2 column_type_2 (column_size_2),
> column_name_3 column_type_3 (column_size_3),
> PRIMARY KEY (column_1, column_n)
> )
> ```

For example:

```
DROP TABLE MODELS;
CREATE TABLE MODELS (
BRAND TEXT (30),
MODEL TEXT (100),
CYLINDER_CAPACITY TEXT (10),
CONSUMPTION TEXT (15),
PRIMARY KEY (BRAND, MODEL)
);
```

This time, the key icon appears in the columns **BRAND** and **MODEL**.

Now we are going to see if the constraint works correctly by executing different **INSERT INTO**:

```
INSERT INTO MODELS (BRAND, MODEL)
VALUES ('SEAT', 'IBIZA 1.4 TDI')
```

It works correctly because it is the first row.

```
INSERT INTO MODELS (BRAND, MODEL)
VALUES ('RENAULT', 'IBIZA 1.4 TDI')
```

This time, the second query does work because, although the model 'IBIZA 1.4 TDI' is repeated, the brand is different in both rows: one is 'SEAT' and the other is 'RENAULT'.

If we execute the same query again, it will fail with an error message.

```
INSERT INTO MODELOS (MARCA, MODELO)
VALUES ('RENAULT', 'IBIZA 1.4 TDI')
```

```
UNIQUE constraint failed: MODELOS.MARCA, MODELOS.MODELO:
INSERT INTO MODELOS (MARCA, MODELO) VALUES ('RENAULT',
'IBIZA 1.4 TDI')
```

- **Adding PRIMARY KEY after creating a table:** if we have already created our table and we need to establish the primary key, we can use a new variant of the query ALTER TABLE.

 **¡IMPORTANT!**

```
ALTER TABLE table_name
ADD PRIMARY KEY (column_1, column_n)
```

SQLite only allows us to add constraints when creating the tables, so this option is not compatible. In any case, an example would be:

```
ALTER TABLE CUSTOMERS
ADD PRIMARY KEY (ID)
```

- **Deleting PRIMARY KEY:** This option is useful either to definitely delete the PK of a table or to modify it since SQL does not enable us to do it directly. If we want other columns to form the PK, we have to delete it first and later create it again.

 **¡IMPORTANT!**

```
ALTER TABLE table_name
DROP PRIMARY KEY
```

As well as in the previous example, SQLite is not compatible with this option. An example of its use would be:

```
ALTER TABLE MODEL
DROP PRIMARY KEY
```

Chapter 2.5
Basic Select

In this chapter:

1. *You will use the query SELECT to read the rows of a table.*

2. *You will combine its use with DISTINCT to look for different values and with COUNT to count rows.*

3. *You will order the results thanks to ORDER BY.*

4. *You will limit the rows to obtain with LIMIT*

What information is there in my database?

As we have commented sometimes during the course, the main functions of a database are storing and bringing back information. In the previous chapters, you have learnt to create tables and to insert rows in them. Well, in this one you will learn to request for data from a database with the use of the sentence SELECT.

Its syntax is the following:

 **¡IMPORTANT!**

SELECT **column_1, column_n**
FROM **table_name**

- SELECT: we indicate the database that we are going to look for information.

- **column_x**: separated by commas, the names of the columns whose data we want to obtain. To select all of them, we can use the asterisk symbol (*).

- FROM: it indicates the end of the list of fields and the beginning of the list of tables (just one for the moment).

- **table_name**: table from which we want to read data.

This is, without doubt, the most powerful keyword of SQL since it accepts plenty of variants, so in the book we will devote some chapters to it. This is focused on its most basic form: the one that lets us have access to the data of only one table.

First, we indicate which columns we want to read and later, the table from which we will extract the information.

To check all the content of the table **CUSTOMERS** we just have to execute:

```
SELECT * FROM CUSTOMERS
```

We can "translate" this query as an order to the database manager:

"Look for all the information you have about all the **CUSTOMERS***"*

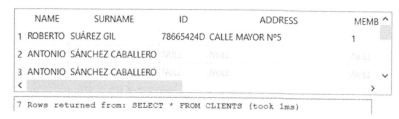

Result of the query.

Or we can also check a set of fields in particular:

```
SELECT NAME, SURNAME, ID
FROM CUSTOMERS
```

"Look for **NAME***,* **ID** *and* **SURNAME** *from all the* **CUSTOMERS***"*

As you have already checked with these two examples, the basic syntax of SELECT is very simple, but it is limited to concrete questions. What happens if what we want to look for is knowing how many customers there are in the database or the different registered addresses?

To be able to do these and many other questions, SQL provides us with words such as COUNT or DISTINCT that complement the query SELECT.

DISTINCT

As its name shows, this query enables us to calculate the different values of a set of columns.

Its syntax is:

 **¡IMPORTANT!**

SELECT DISTINCT **column_1, column_n**
FROM **table_name**

- **SELECT DISTINCT**: we indicate the database that we want to look for unique values.

- **column_x**: separated by commas, the names of the columns. To use all of them we can use the asterisk symbol (*).

- **FROM**.

- **table_name**.

For example, to obtain a list with the names of our customers:

SELECT DISTINCT **NAME**
FROM **CUSTOMERS**

We can also use a set of columns:

SELECT DISTINCT **TEL_NUMBER, ADDRESS**
FROM **CUSTOMERS**

TEL_NUMBER	ADDRESS
679867456	CALLE MAYOR Nº5
NULL	NULL
NULL	Calle Manuela Malasaña 23. Madrid

As you can see in the results, for SQLite NULL is a value and therefore, it is used when generating the combinations of different telephones and addresses.

If we check the results with all the values of the table:

SELECT **TEL_NUMBER, ADDRESS**
FROM **CUSTOMERS**

ROW NUMBER	TEL_NUMBER	ADDRESS
1	679867456	CALLE MAYOR Nº5
2	NULL	NULL
3	NULL	NULL
4	NULL	NULL
5	NULL	Calle Manuela Malasaña 23. Madrid
6	NULL	NULL
7	NULL	NULL

The first row of the query DISTINCT corresponds to the first of the table **CUSTOMERS**. On the other hand, the second row corresponds to the rows number 2, 3, 4, 6 and 7 while row number 3 corresponds to number 5.

ORDER BY

Apart from asking for information to the database, we can also indicate it in which order we want to receive the rows. If, for example, we need to show all the entries of a blog, the normal thing would be getting back first the most current posts. To do this, we will use the query ORDER BY at the end of any SELECT query.

For example:

NAME	SURNAME
ANTONIO	SÁNCHEZ CABALLERO
ANTONIO	SÁNCHEZ CABALLERO
ANTONIO	SÁNCHEZ CABALLERO
HÉCTOR	GARCÍA PASCUAL
LAURA	MARÍN SÁNCHEZ
ROBERTO	SUÁREZ GIL
SILVIA	ROMERO FERNÁNDEZ

SELECT **NAME, SURNAME**
FROM **CUSTOMERS** ORDER BY **NAME**

This, translated to our language would be:

*"Look for the name and surname of the **CUSTOMERS** and order them by **NAME**"*.

We can use one or some columns. In this case, the database would order by the first column and if two rows have the same value, it would continue with the second column and so on.

We can also decide by each column, if we want a descending (DESC) or ascending (ASC) order, being this one the criterion by default.

Try executing:

```
SELECT NAME, SURNAME
FROM CUSTOMERS ORDER BY NAME ASC
```

You will see that there is no difference in using ASC or not. However, try this:

```
SELECT NAME, SURNAME
FROM CUSTOMERS ORDER BY NAME DESC
```

NAME	SURNAME
SILVIA	ROMERO FERNÁNDEZ
ROBERTO	SUÁREZ GIL
LAURA	MARÍN SÁNCHEZ
HÉCTOR	GARCÍA PASCUAL
ANTONIO	SÁNCHEZ CABALLERO
ANTONIO	SÁNCHEZ CABALLERO
ANTONIO	SÁNCHEZ CABALLERO

LIMIT

With this keyword, you can indicate the database that you only want to get back the first rows of a query.

 ¡IMPORTANT!

```
SELECT [...]
LIMIT row_number
```

- SELECT: query.

- LIMIT: we indicate the database that we are going to establish a limit of rows.

- row_number: númber of rows to show.

For example, to show the three oldest customers you could execute:

```
SELECT *
FROM CUSTOMERS
ORDER BY AGE DESC LIMIT 3
```

COUNT

Up to now, the queries we have done were focused on getting back the content of a table. This means, having a look at the data that each row contains.

If we only want to know just how many customers have been registered or how many have given us their telephone number, we can use COUNT:

 ¡IMPORTANT!

> SELECT COUNT (* / **column** / DISTINCT **column**)
> FROM **table_name**

- SELECT.

- COUNT (* / **column** / DISTINCT **column**):
  - COUNT (*): count rows.
  - COUNT (**column**): count rows that have a value in the specified column. This means that the column is not NULL.
  - COUNT (DISTINCT **column**): count different values (rows with NULL value are disregarded).

- FROM.

- **table_name**.

We are going to see an example of each option of COUNT:

> SELECT COUNT (*)
> FROM **CUSTOMERS**

The result is 7 since this is the number of rows in the table.

> SELECT COUNT (**ID**)
> FROM **CUSTOMERS**

Since there are only two customers who have reported their ID, the result of the query is two.

> SELECT COUNT (DISTINCT **NAME**)
> FROM **CUSTOMERS**

The database gives us five that correspond to the names: ROBERTO, ANTONIO (it is repeated three times but as there is a DISTINCT, it only counts as one), HÉCTOR, SILVIA and LAURA.

 **EXERCISES**

Write the queries that correspond to the following questions:

- How many customers have given us their telephone number?
- Which are the ages of the customers?
- What are the names and surnames of all our customers?
- Suppose that we want to send them a happy birthday card in their birthdays, how many cards do we need to buy?
- When were they born?

Solution:

```
SELECT COUNT (TEL_NUMBER)
FROM CUSTOMERS;

SELECT DISTINCT AGE
FROM CUSTOMERS;

SELECT NAME, SURNAME
FROM CLIENTES;

SELECT COUNT (BIRTH_DATE)
FROM CUSTOMERS;

SELECT DISTINCT BIRTH_DATE
FROM CUSTOMERS;
```

Capítulo 2.6
Select + Where

In this chapter:

> 1. *You will learn to use* WHERE *to limit the set of rows given back by a* SELECT *query.*
>
> 2. *You will use simple operators such as* >, <, = *together with others more complex such as* BETWEEN, IN *or* IS NULL.
>
> 3. *You will combine some of them thanks to the logical operators* AND, NOT *and* OR.

Looking for rows

Except for the examples of LIMIT, all the queries that we have seen in the previous chapters had access to the complete content of a table. It means, when we looked for a subset of rows of the table **CUSTOMERS**, the database gave us back the information of all the rows.

This is not a problem when we are working with tables with a few rows but obviously, this is not viable if we need to manipulate hundreds, thousands or millions of rows.

Moreover, not always will we want to have access to all the data. Think, for example, of the front page of a blog. The normal thing is that not all the entries of the webpage appear there, but only the first ten or twenty. Or, if we are having a look at a concrete post, usually only the comments of that article appear.

Well, to limit the set of rows to read in a SELECT query, we will use the word WHERE after the list of tables. For example:

```
SELECT * FROM CUSTOMERS
WHERE NAME = 'ANTONIO'
```

Translated to our language:

*"Look for all the information of the **CUSTOMERS** whose name is **ANTONIO**".*

To build the filter condition, we will use comparisons, mathematical operators and logical operators. In the following sections, you will find explanations and examples of the most common ones.

Simple comparisons

The most usual thing is to look for rows in which one or some columns fulfil a determined filter condition:

- Customers with the **ID** 23232323A.
- Products with lower price than 100 €.
- Films in the "Action" category.

To build them, SQL has the following simple operators:

OPERATOR	MEANING	EXAMPLE	MEANING
=	Equal to	ID = '23232323A'	Look for customers with the ID 23232323A
!= ó <>	Not equal to	GENRE != 'Terror'	Look for films that are not Horror ones
>	Greater than	PRICE > 100	Look for products with a price higher than 100 € (from 101 €)
<	Less than	PRICE < 50	Look for products with a cost price than 50 € (up to 49 €)
>=	Greater than or Equal to	PRICE >= 100	Look for products with a price of 100 € or higher
<=	Less than or Equal to	PRICE <= 50	Look for products with a cost of 50 € or lower

To take into account:

- Remember that when you want to use text in a query, you always need to delimit it with simple inverted commas.

- The numeric comparisons "greater than", "less than", etc. are done naturally, which means that the lower numbers are the negative ones and the higher ones the positive.

- The database usually takes into account if a text is written in capital letters or lower cases, for example, "Madrid" is different from "MADRID".

- The columns with a null value are disregarded with these operators. This means that if we look for customers who are older than 18, we will only obtain those who have a value in age and who are older than 18.

• •

 EXERCISES

Try to create and execute the following queries:

- Name of the customers whose ID is 78665424D.
- ID of the customers whose ID is not 78665424D
- All the data of the customers whose name is SILVIA.

- Number of customers older than 35.
- Customers with more than 10 points in descending order of points.

Solution:

```
SELECT NAME
FROM CUSTOMERS
WHERE ID = '78665424D';
```

```
SELECT ID
FROM CUSTOMERS
WHERE ID != '78665424D';
```

```
SELECT *
FROM CUSTOMERS
WHERE NAME = 'SILVIA';
```

```
SELECT COUNT (*)
FROM CUSTOMERS
WHERE AGE > 35;
```

```
SELECT *
FROM CUSTOMERS
WHERE POINTS = 10
ORDER BY POINTS DESC;
```

• •

BETWEEN

Palabra clave que nos permite buscar filas en base a un rango de valores. Es equivalente al uso de los operadores <= y >= en la misma condición.

 **¡IMPORTANT!**

column BETWEEN *value_1* AND *value_2*

- **column**: numeric column whose value we are going to compare.

- BETWEEN

- *value_1*: lower limit of the range. Minimum value that the column can have to fulfil the condition.

- AND

- *value_2*: upper limit of the range.

To check if it works, execute the following:

```
SELECT NAME, AGE
FROM CUSTOMERS
WHERE AGE BETWEEN 32 AND 45
```

NAME	AGE
ROBERTO	32
LAURA	45

The first value must be always inferior to the second. If it is not like this, the database will not give us back any result. You can check it with the query:

```
SELECT NAME, AGE
FROM CUSTOMERS
WHERE AGE BETWEEN 45 AND 32
```

IN

If what we want to look for is a set of values (numeric or not), instead of using several times the comparison "=" we can use IN whose syntax is:

 ¡IMPORTANT!

column IN (*value_1, value_2*)

- **column**: column whose value we are going to look for.

- IN

- (*value_1, value_2*): set of values that are going to be looked for.

```
SELECT NAME, SURNAME
FROM CUSTOMERS
WHERE NAME IN ('ANTONIO', 'SILVIA')
```

NAME	SURNAME
ANTONIO	SÁNCHEZ CABALLERO
ANTONIO	SÁNCHEZ CABALLERO
SILVIA	ROMERO FERNÁNDEZ
ANTONIO	SÁNCHEZ CABALLERO

Logical operators

Although it is common to look for rows based on just one column, we will be forced many times to make queries that involve some attributes.

Think, for example, when you are surfing an online shop. The normal thing is that you want to see products of a specific category (TVs, for instance) with a maximum price (900 €) and maybe you need to restrict the search to your favourite brands.

To be able to make those queries, we have two logical operators: AND and OR. Both of them "join" two conditions in the following way:

¡IMPORTANT!

condition_1 AND / OR *condition_2*

- *condition_1*.

- AND / OR:
  - AND: both conditions must be fulfilled. For example: "I want to look for watches that are aquatic and with a chronograph".
  - OR: it is enough if one condition is fulfilled: "I want to look for watches that are aquatic or with a chronograph".

- *condition_2*.

Let's see an example of each case:

```
SELECT NAME, BIRTH_DATE
FROM CUSTOMERS
WHERE NAME = 'ANTONIO'
OR BIRTH_DATE = '1968-06-05'
```

"Look for all the customers whose name is ANTONIO or who were born on 5th June 1968".

NAME	SURNAME
ANTONIO	NULL
ANTONIO	NULL
ANTONIO	*1968-06-05*

Three rows are shown. The two first ones only fulfil the name = 'ANTONIO' whereas the third one fulfils both conditions.

However, if we use AND:

```
SELECT NAME, BIRTH_DATE
FROM CUSTOMERS
WHERE NAME = 'ANTONIO'
AND BIRTH_DATE = '1968-06-05'
```

NAME	BIRTH_DATE
ANTONIO	1968-06-05

SQLite only gives us back one row since it is the only one that fulfils both conditions.

IS NULL

Operator used to check if a field is null. Its syntax is very simple:

¡IMPORTANT!

column IS NULL

- **column**: column in which we will carry out the check.
- IS NULL

```
SELECT NAME, ID
FROM CUSTOMERS
WHERE ID IS NULL
```

NAME	ID
ANTONIO	NULL
ANTONIO	NULL
HÉCTOR	NULL
LAURA	NULL
ANTONIO	NULL

NOT

It reverses the sense of a condition and so, it must be used in combination with a simple operator (>, <, =...), complex (IN, BETWEEN, IS NULL) or logical (AND, OR).

OPERATOR	SINTAXIS	EXAMPLE
= != ó <> < > >= <=	NOT column_1 operador **column_2**	NOT AGE > 18
BETWEEN IN	NOT operator	NOT IN ('Horror', 'Action')
IS NULL	column_1 IS NOT NULL	ID IS NOT NULL

Try to execute the following queries and compare the results.

```
SELECT *
FROM CUSTOMERS
WHERE AGE != 32;

SELECT *
FROM CUSTOMERS
WHERE NOT AGE != 32;
```

```
SELECT *
FROM CUSTOMERS
WHERE AGE BETWEEN 18 AND 25;

SELECT *
FROM CUSTOMERS
WHERE AGE NOT BETWEEN 18 AND 25;
```

```
SELECT *
FROM CUSTOMERS
WHERE ID IS NULL;

SELECT *
FROM CUSTOMERS
WHERE ID IS NOT NULL;
```

```
SELECT *
FROM CUSTOMERS
WHERE NAME IN ('ROBERTO', 'ANTONIO');

SELECT *
FROM CUSTOMERS
WHERE NAME NOT IN ('ROBERTO', 'ANTONIO');
```

Use of parentheses

Before finishing this section, we are going to make things a little bit more difficult using parentheses. As in algebra, its function is grouping conditions so that they are first evaluated together.

For example:

```
SELECT NAME, BIRTH_DATE, AGE
FROM CUSTOMERS
WHERE
(NAME = 'ANTONIO' AND BIRTH_DATE = '1968-06-05') OR
(NAME != 'ANTONIO' AND AGE > 40)
```

"Look for those customers whose name is Antonio and who have been born on 5th June 1968 or whose name is not Antonio and they are older than 40".

NAME	BIRTH_DATE	AGE
LAURA	NULL	45
ANTONIO	1968-06-05	NULL

The first row fulfils the condition "whose name is not Antonio and they are older than 40" Whereas the second one fulfils the condition "whose name is Antonio and who have been born on the 5th of June".

You must use them in all the queries that include operators AND and OR at the same time since otherwise you could obtain unexpected results.

To check this, we are going to try to look for the following:

"Look for all the customers that are not Roberto with a membership number = 1".

```
SELECT NAME, MEMBER_NUM
FROM CUSTOMERS
WHERE
NOT (NAME = 'ROBERTO' AND MEMBER_NUM = 1)
```

However, if we write the query without parentheses, we will not obtain any rows.

NAME	MEMBER_NUM
ROBERTO	1
HÉCTOR	123
SILVIA	NULL
LAURA	NULL

```
SELECT NAME, BIRTH_DATE
FROM CUSTOMERS
WHERE
NOT NAME = 'ROBERTO' AND MEMBER_NUM = 1
```

This is because when the parentheses are removed, the operator NOT only affects the first condition, which means that what we are really doing is:

```
SELECT *
FROM CUSTOMERS
WHERE NAME != 'ROBERTO' AND MEMBER_NUM = 1
```

"Look for all the customers whose name is not Roberto and who have a membership number = 1".

Congratulations! You have just finished one of the most difficult lessons of the course. It has been tough but thanks to it, you are ready to ask the most frequently asked questions to a database.

• •

 **EXERCISES**

To finish, try writing the following queries:

- Number of customers who are older than 30.
- Obtain customers whose names are Héctor or Laura, or whose names are neither Héctor nor Laura and whose telephone number is 679867456.
- Customers with ID 78665424D, membership number higher than 0 and older than 18 years old.
- Number of customers without ID.
- Customers whose age is between 10 and 35 and who have provided their email address when they registered.

Solution:

```
SELECT COUNT (*)
FROM CUSTOMERS
WHERE AGE > 30;

SELECT *
FROM CUSTOMERS
WHERE
(NAME IN ('HECTOR', 'LAURA')) OR
(NAME NOT IN ('HECTOR', 'LAURA')
AND TEL_NUMBER = 679867456);

SELECT *
FROM CUSTOMERS
WHERE ID = '78665424D'
AND MEMBER_NUM > 0 AND AGE > 18;

SELECT COUNT (*)
FROM CUSTOMERS
WHERE ID IS NULL;

SELECT *
FROM CUSTOMERS
WHERE AGE BETWEEN 10
AND 35 AND EMAIL IS NOT NULL;
```

• •

Chapter 2.7
Join

In this chapter:

> *1. You will blend the data from different tables using the query JOIN.*
>
> *2. You will combine its use with WHERE to create complex queries.*

Relating information

Up to now, all the previously seen queries have affected a single table. Although this is perfectly normal when creating or modifying them, it is not so when we talk about requesting data from a database.

Databases were born to structure and organise data, so if we want to separate the personal information of our customers from their purchase history, we will need at least two tables: one with the customers data and other with the orders.

Now think that you need to obtain a relation of all the orders done this month altogether with the ID numbers of the purchasers. With the keywords that you have learnt up to now, you would need two queries:

- One to **CUSTOMERS** table to obtain the **ID** of all of them.

- Another to the purchase history.

It can be a good option since they are only two queries. But, what if you need to get access to five tables? Wouldn't it be better to query them at the same time? Well, to join some tables in the same SQL query, the language provides us with the keyword JOIN.

As its name shows, this query lets us join two tables using columns as "glue". It can be represented visually in the following way:

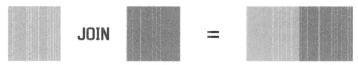

Graphic representation of a JOIN.

Imagine we have the following tables:

Table CUSTOMERS:

MEMBER_NUM	ID	NAME
1	78665424D	ROBERTO SUÁREZ GIL
2	78665432Q	ANTONIO SÁNCHEZ CABALLERO
3	85691345U	LAURA MARÍN SÁNCHEZ

Table ORDERS:

MEMBER_NUM	DATE	PRODUCT	QUANTITY
1	01/02/2015	Table	1
1	02/02/2015	Chair	4
1	02/09/2015	Lamp	4
2	02/10/2015	Carpet	3

As what we want to obtain is a list of orders together with the **ID** of the purchasers, what we really need is to "glue" in the **ORDERS** table the **ID** of the **CUSTOMERS**.

To do this, we need to link both tables with at least one column that will be the connecting link of both. In this case, it would be the **MEMBER_NUM**, which is both in the table **CUSTOMERS** (to identify each of them) and in the **ORDERS** (to indicate which customer bought each product).

So, the JOIN will consist in adding to each row of the table **ORDERS** the **ID** of register of the **CUSTOMER** who has the same value in the column **MEMBER_NUM**:

MEMBER_NUM	DATE	PRODUCT	QUANTITY	ID
1	01/02/2015	Table	1	78665424D
1	02/02/2015	Chair	4	78665424D
1	02/09/2015	Lamp	4	78665424D
2	02/10/2015	Carpet	3	78665432Q

The logic that SQLite follows row by row is:

- Look in the table **CUSTOMERS** for the row with the same **MEMBER_NUM** of **ORDERS**.

- It reads the attribute **ID** and this is added to the results together with the rest of the data from the row of **ORDERS**.

Its syntax is the following:

```
SELECT ORDERS.MEMBER_NUM,
       ORDERS.DATE,
       ORDERS.PRODUCT,
       ORDERS.QUANTITY,
       CUSTOMERS.ID
FROM ORDERS
JOIN CUSTOMERS ON
ORDERS.MEMBER_NUM = CUSTOMERS.MEMBER_NUM
```

Following this syntax, the query of the example would be:

- Since we are using several tables, we need to indicate to SQLite the origin of each column because, for example, **MEMBER_NUM** is in both tables.

- For this, we add the name of the table and a stop (.) as prefix of the name of the column. For example, "**ORDERS.MEMBER_NUM**" represents the column **MEMBER_NUM** of the table **ORDERS**.

- The "master" table is the one that appears before the JOIN and the detail, that means, the one that contains additional data, which will be specified later.

- Although it is not the normal thing, the condition that goes after the ON can be as complex as we need, including arithmetic or logical operators, parentheses, etc.

But, before starting practising with the query JOIN, it is good to stop for a while and see the use of the alias to simplify and reduce the queries that we are going to use from now on.

Use of an alias to name objects

As we have just seen, we can use the name of a table as prefix to indicate SQLite the table from which a data must be read.

This is practical when the names are short and meaningful or when we use a few tables and/or columns. But, if the number grows or the names are too long, everything becomes more complicated.

To reduce the size of the queries, SQL lets us use an alias, which means, a temporal name that we can assign to both tables and columns.

Its syntax is:

¡IMPORTANT!

table / column AS alias

- 🔊 **table / column**: original name.

- 🔊 **AS**: optional keyword, it means, we can assign the alias without using it.

- 🔊 **alias**: temporal name to be used in replacement of original name.

Let's see an example without alias and another with it:

```
SELECT CUSTOMERS.NAME, CUSTOMERS.SURNAME
FROM CUSTOMERS
```

To reduce the size of the query we can use the alias "C":

```
SELECT C.NAME, C.SURNAME
FROM CUSTOMERS C
```

Finally, an example using an alias also in the columns and the keyword AS:

```
SELECT C.NAME, C.SURNAME AS COMPLETE_SURNAME
FROM CUSTOMERS C
```

NAME	COMPLETE_SURNAME
ROBERTO	SUÁREZ GIL
ANTONIO	SÁNCHEZ CABALLERO
ANTONIO	SÁNCHEZ CABALLERO
HÉCTOR	GARCÍA PASCUAL
SILVIA	ROMERO FERNÁNDEZ
LAURA	MARÍN SÁNCHEZ
ANTONIO	SÁNCHEZ CABALLERO

As you can see in the results grid, SQLite shows us the data using the name of the column **COMPLETE_SURNAME** instead of **SURNAME**.

Practising the query JOIN

Now we are going to increase our model to be able to carry out some tests of the query use.

First, we will store new customers.

```
INSERT INTO CUSTOMERS (MEMBER_NUM, NAME, ID, AGE)
VALUES (1000, 'JUAN','03498734R',25);

INSERT INTO CUSTOMERS (MEMBER_NUM, NAME, ID, AGE)
VALUES (1001, 'MARÍA','40118730J',55);

INSERT INTO CUSTOMERS (MEMBER_NUM, NAME, ID, AGE)
VALUES (1002, 'ROBERTO','345173900',27);
```

Later, we will create a table of **ORDERS**:

```
CREATE TABLE ORDERS (
    MEMBER_NUM INTEGER (4),
    DATE DATETIME,
    PRODUCT TEXT (100),
    QUANTITY INTEGER (4))
```

Finally, we will insert some rows as an example.

```
INSERT INTO ORDERS (MEMBER_NUM, DATE, PRODUCT, QUANTITY)
VALUES (1000, '2015-01-12', 'CANDLE', 5);

INSERT INTO ORDERS (MEMBER_NUM, DATE, PRODUCT, QUANTITY)
VALUES (1000, '2015-02-14', 'CANDLE', 5);

INSERT INTO ORDERS (MEMBER_NUM, DATE, PRODUCT, QUANTITY)
VALUES (1000, '2015-06-20', 'PHOTO FRAME', 2);

INSERT INTO ORDERS (MEMBER_NUM, DATE, PRODUCT, QUANTITY)
VALUES (1001, '2015-02-18', 'PHOTO FRAME', 1);

INSERT INTO ORDERS (MEMBER_NUM, DATE, PRODUCT, QUANTITY)
VALUES (1001, '2015-10-09', 'CUP', 1);

INSERT INTO ORDERS (MEMBER_NUM, DATE, PRODUCT, QUANTITY)
VALUES (1002, '2015-12-10', 'WALL CLOCK', 1);
```

Now that we have tables and data, we can start practising. We will start with the example at the beginning of the chapter: *"All the orders together with the **ID** of the purchaser"*.

```
SELECT V.*, C.ID
FROM ORDERS V
JOIN CUSTOMERS C ON V.MEMBER_NUM = C.MEMBER_NUM
```

Remember, "*" after SELECT indicates the database that we want to read all the columns. In the example, we use the prefix **V** to obtain all from the table **ORDERS**.

MEMBER_NUM	DATE	PRODUCT	QUANTITY	ID
1000	12/01/2015	CANDLE	5	03498734R
1000	14/02/2015	CANDLE	5	03498734R
1000	20/06/2015	PHOTO FRAME	2	03498734R
1001	18/02/2015	PHOTO FRAME	1	40118730J
1001	09/10/2015	CUP	1	40118730J
1002	10/12/2015	WALL CLOCK	1	345173900

Now, we will look for the *"Name of the customers who have bought cups"*. To do this, we will combine JOIN with the word WHERE:

```
SELECT C.NAME
FROM ORDERS V
JOIN CUSTOMERS C ON V.MEMBER_NUM = C.MEMBER_NUM
WHERE V.PRODUCT = 'CUP'
```

NAME
MARÍA

As with SELECT, we need to add the prefix to the columns that intervene in the condition WHERE.

Imagine that we need to know now *"all the data of the members who have bought once"*.

```
SELECT DISTINCT C.*
FROM ORDERS V
JOIN CUSTOMERS C ON V.MEMBER_NUM = C.NUM_SOCIO
```

NAME	SURNAME	ID	ADDRESS	MEMBER_NUM
JUAN	NULL	03498734R	NULL	1000
MARÍA	NULL	40118730J	NULL	1001
ROBERTO	NULL	345173900	NULL	1002

Have a look that we did not need to do anything to select "who have bought once". This is because JOIN only shows the data when the joining condition is fulfilled and as we commented in the chapter dedicated to WHERE, the empty values are never taken into account in the arithmetic operators =, >, <...

This implies that fo example, in the query only members with orders and orders with a value in **MEMBER_NUM** are selected. If a purchase had been associated with a customer outside the customers table, it would not have been shown in the previous query.

And, to finish, imagine that what we need to know is how many customers, older than 20, have purchased photo frames. To do this, we will add the keywords COUNT and DISTINCT.

```
SELECT COUNT (DISTINCT C.MEMBER_NUM) AS NUM_CUSTOMERS
FROM ORDERS V
JOIN CUSTOMERS C ON V.MEMBER_NUM = C.MEMBER_NUM
WHERE V.PRODUCT = 'PHOTO FRAME'
AND C.AGE > 20
```

NUM_CUSTOMERS
2

- First, we have mixed the tables of orders and customers to associate with each customer the products bought.

- We filter the product "photo frame" and the age older than 20 thanks to the query WHERE.

- Finally, we count the different customers with COUNT DISTINCT.

- For the result to be more legible, we use the alias "**NUM_CUSTOMERS**"

EXERCISES

Write the following SQL queries:

- **ID** of the customers who have bought candles.
- Number of customers, younger than 50, who have bought clocks.
- Number of orders done by customers older than 25.

Solution:

```
SELECT DISTINCT (C.ID)
FROM ORDERS V
JOIN CUSTOMERS C ON V.MEMBER_NUM = C.MEMBER_NUM
WHERE V.PRODUCT = 'CANDLE';

SELECT COUNT (DISTINCT C.MEMBER_NUM) AS NUM_CUSTOMERS
FROM ORDERS V
JOIN CUSTOMERS C ON V.MEMBER_NUM = C.MEMBER_NUM
WHERE V.PRODUCT = 'WALL CLOCK'
AND AGE < 50;

SELECT COUNT (*) AS NUM_ORDERS
FROM ORDERS V
JOIN CUSTOMERS C ON V.MEMBER_NUM = C. MEMBER_NUM
WHERE AGE < 25;
```

Chapter 2.8
Union and Except

In this chapter:

> *1. You will blend the results of two queries thanks to UNION.*
>
> *2. You will learn the difference between UNION and UNION ALL.*
>
> *3. You will use EXCEPT to subtract results.*

Addition of results: UNION

Imagine now, that we have built a database for a business that has both a physical shop and an online shop and that we have separated into two independent tables.

If we want to obtain a list of people who have registered in both businesses, we can use the query JOIN that visually can be represented as an intersection of two sets:

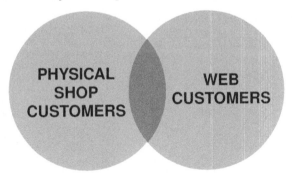

Representation of the operation JOIN.

The result would be those customers who appear in both tables.

Now suppose that what we want to obtain is a list with all the customers, no matter where they are registered. To do this, we need to "join" the content of two queries: the one of the customers of the physical shop and the one of the customers of the web, which visually can be represented as:

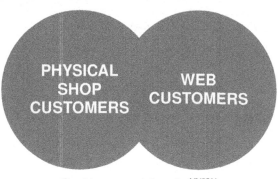

Graphic representation of a UNION.

To do this operation, SQL provides us with the keyword UNION which syntax is:

> ### 🗨 ¡IMPORTANT!
>
> *query_1* UNION / UNION ALL
> *query_2* UNION / UNION ALL
> *query_n*
>
> - *query_1*: SQL query to one or more tables. It must have the same columns as the rest
>
> - UNION / UNION ALL:
>   - UNION: it adds the result of the queries using DISTINCT, which means if the same element appears in several queries, it only appears once in the result.
>   - UNION ALL: it adds all the results.
>
> - *query_1, query_n*: SQL query to one or more tables. It must have the same columns as the rest.

Let's create a new table for on-line customers:

```
CREATE TABLE WEB_CUSTOMERS (
MEMBER_NUM INTEGER (4),
NAME TEXT (40),
ID TEXT (9));
INSERT INTO WEB_CUSTOMERS VALUES (1000, 'JUAN', '03498734R');
INSERT INTO WEB_CUSTOMERS VALUES (1006, 'AINHOA', '29401459I');
INSERT INTO WEB_CUSTOMERS VALUES (1001, 'MARÍA', '40118730J');
```

To obtain a list with all the customers, we can execute:

```
SELECT MEMBER_NUM, ID, NAME FROM CUSTOMERS
UNION ALL
SELECT MEMBER_NUM, ID, NAME FROM WEB_CUSTOMERS
```

As you can see in the results grid, the members 1000 and 1001 appear twice because they are registered both in **CUSTOMERS** and in **WEB_CUSTOMERS**.

However, if we use the query UNION they will only appear once since the database is in charge of deleting repeated results:

```
SELECT MEMBER_NUM, ID, NAME FROM CUSTOMERS
UNION
SELECT MEMBER_NUM, ID, NAME FROM WEB_CUSTOMERS
```

Subtraction of results: EXCEPT

Now imagine that what we want to obtain is a list of customers of the physical shop who have not registered in the online business yet in order to send them, for example, some type of discount to encourage them to enter into the web.

For this, the logical thing would be to subtract the customers of the shop who have also registered online. It means:

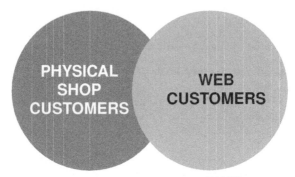

Representation of the operation EXCEPT.

The result would be the dark part of the set "**PHYSICAL SHOP CUSTOMERS**".

SQL allows us to do this operation with the query EXCEPT (or MINUS that is the name given to this operation in other databases) whose syntax is very similar to UNION:

¡IMPORTANT!

> *query_1* EXCEPT
> *query_2* EXCEPT
> *query_n*

- *query_1*: query to one or more tables. It must have the same columns as the rest.

- EXCEPT: subtraction of results.

- *query_2*, *query_n*: SQL query to one or more tables. It must have the same columns as the rest.

To do the operation of the example we must execute:

```
SELECT MEMBER_NUM, ID, NAME FROM CUSTOMERS
EXCEPT
SELECT MEMBER_NUM, ID, NAME FROM WEB_CUSTOMERS
```

MEMBER_NUM	ID	NAME
NULL	NULL	ANTONIO
NULL	NULL	LAURA
NULL	78665432Q	SILVIA
1	78665424D	ROBERTO
123	NULL	HÉCTOR
1002	345173900	ROBERTO

Chapter 2.9

Update and Delete

In this chapter:

> *1. You will learn to modify the values of the rows that already exist in the database thanks to UPDATE.*
>
> *2. You will delete concrete rows of a table using the keyword DELETE.*
>
> *3. You will accept or reject the changes with COMMIT and ROLLBACK.*
>
> *4. You will manage transactions with the keyword BEGIN TRANSACTION.*

Modifying the content of the database

Apart from storing and consulting information, a database must allow us to modify the rows that are already stored in the tables. For example, think when you change the shipping data in an online shop or when you update the credit card number.

In order to make these operations, SQL uses the operators UPDATE (to change) and DELETE (to delete) that are normally used in combination with the keyword WHERE, since to alter or delete any data, we need to locate it first.

This nuance is important because when you insert rows there is no risk of modifying anything, but if we make a mistake when selecting them in an update, we can lose information.

To minimize this risk, the databases implement a mechanism that is called "transaction" and it consists basically in the fact that any modification made with INSERT, UPDATE or DELETE must be confirmed with the query COMMIT in order to be effective.

This query is executed when we press on the option "Write Changes" of SQLite.

On the other hand, if we make a mistake we can use the query ROLLBACK that makes just the opposite: it reverts the changes, so it corresponds to the option "Revert Changes".

Before continuing, and to avoid accidents, it is advisable to backup database file (MYSHOP.sqlite3).

DELETE

The syntax to delete rows from a database is:

 **¡IMPORTANT!**

DELETE FROM **table** <WHERE>

- DELETE FROM: we indicate the database that we are going to delete rows from a table.

- **table**: affected table.

- WHERE: search conditions that must be fulfilled by the rows. It is optional, but if we do not specify it, all the rows of the table will be deleted.

Let's check the functioning of this query. First, we count the rows of **CUSTOMERS** table:

SELECT COUNT (*) FROM **CUSTOMERS**

In our case, the result is 10. Next, we delete the ones with no **ID**.

DELETE FROM **CUSTOMERS** WHERE **ID** IS NULL

Now, we count the rows of the table again. The result is 5.

Then, we try to delete those who are older than 30.

DELETE FROM **CUSTOMERS** WHERE **AGE** > *30*

There are three remaining rows in the table.

Finally, we delete all the remaining rows so that the table would be empty.

DELETE FROM **CUSTOMERS**

As we have seen at the beginning, to revert all these changes, we can use the query ROLLBACK. Simply, write it in the SQL editor and execute it.

If you go back to check the table CUSTOMERS, you will see that it has 10 rows again.

UPDATE

The functioning is very similar to DELETE, but in this query, apart from locating the rows to be modified, we must specify the new values.

 **¡IMPORTANT!**

UPDATE table SET assignments <WHERE>

- **UPDATE**: instruction that indicates the database that we are going to modify rows.
- **table**: where we are going to make the changes.
- **SET**
- **assignments**: column = value pairs separated by a comma with which we indicate the new values for the attributes of the table. The values can be fixed (a number, text, etc.), operations (such as adding 10 to a quantity) or they can even refer to other columns of the same row.
- **WHERE**: as well as in DELETE, it is optional but if we do not add any condition, all the rows of the table will be modified.

Let's assign number zero to all those customers who do not have a membership number.

```
UPDATE CUSTOMERS SET MEMBER_NUM = 0
WHERE MEMBER_NUM IS NULL;

SELECT NAME, MEMBER_NUM FROM CUSTOMERS;
```

NAME	MEMBER_NUM
ROBERTO	1
ANTONIO	0
ANTONIO	0
HÉCTOR	123

And, to finish, we revert the changes again.

```
ROLLBACK
```

Transactions

In **DB BROWSER FOR SQLITE** the functioning of UPDATE is slightly different from DE-LETE because although you need to make COMMIT or press the button "Write Changes" to accept changes, these are also accepted if we make a second UPDATE.

What this really means is that by executing two UPDATE queries one after the other is the same as executing UPDATE + COMMIT + UPDATE.

In order to control correctly which changes are saved in the database and which are not, we must use the mechanism of transactions.

A transaction is a set of modifying instructions (INSERT, UPDATE...) that are executed all together as a block, either all of them are accepted (COMMIT) or all are rejected (ROLLBACK).

The syntax is:

 ¡IMPORTANT!

BEGIN TRANSACTION
SQL queries
COMMIT / ROLLBACK

- BEGIN TRANSACTION: we indicate the beginning of the block of instructions.

- *SQL queries*: modifying queries separated by a semicolon ";"

- COMMIT / ROLLBACK: to finish, we accept or reject the changes.

 EXERCISES

To check the functioning of this functionality, we are going to try making the following operations:

- Adding 5 to the age of all the customers.
- Adding 100 points to all the customers who do not have any and are older than 30.
- Counting the customers with at least 1 point.
- Discard the changes.
- Counting again the customers with at least 1 point..

Solution:

```
BEGIN TRANSACTION;
UPDATE CUSTOMERS SET AGE = AGE + 5;
UPDATE CUSTOMERS SET POINTS = 100
WHERE POINTS IS NULL AND AGE > 30;
SELECT COUNT (*) FROM CUSTOMERS WHERE POINTS >= 1;
ROLLBACK;
SELECT COUNT (*) FROM CUSTOMERS
WHERE POINTS >= 1;
```

The first time we count, we will obtain four customers and the second time, after discarding the changes, we will obtain two.

Important, if when executing BEGIN TRANSACTION *you get the following:*

cannot start a transaction within a transaction: BEGIN TRANSACTION;

It means that there is a transaction already open. Execute a ROLLBACK *and start again. It should work perfectly.*

• • • • • • • • • • • • • • • • • •

Try to make queries that solve all the following examples. To avoid risks, please, start all of them with BEGIN TRANSACTION, *finish them with* ROLLBACK *and execute them line by line.*

- Deleting customers without a membership number.
- Assigning as many points to the customers as the membership number they have.
- Assigning to the column **TEL_NUM** the value of **NUM_TEL_LANDLINE** if the first is empty.
- Assigning the membership number 23 to the customer with **ID** 78665432Q.

Solution:

```
BEGIN TRANSACTION;
DELETE FROM CUSTOMERS WHERE MEMBER_NUM IS NULL;
SELECT * FROM CUSTOMERS;
ROLLBACK;

BEGIN TRANSACTION;
UPDATE CUSTOMERS SET POINTS = MEMBER_NUM;
SELECT * FROM CUSTOMERS;
ROLLBACK;
```

```
BEGIN TRANSACTION;
UPDATE CUSTOMERS SET TEL_NUMBER = NUM_TEL_LANDLINE;
WHERE TEL_NUMBER IS NULL;
SELECT * FROM CUSTOMERS;
ROLLBACK;


BEGIN TRANSACTION;
UPDATE CUSTOMERS SET MEMBER_NUM = 23 WHERE ID = '78665432Q';
SELECT * FROM CUSTOMERS;
ROLLBACK;
```

Chapter 2.10
Second day summary

In brief

A hard day but definitely it was worth it.

You have learnt enough, not only to manage and make simple queries to a database, but also to delve into more complex operations such as, for example, the aggregate functions that we will see in the next chapters.

We started the day with the fundaments of the language: keywords, operators, types of data, etc. essential to be able to write SQL queries.

Later, you learnt to create, modify and delete tables, creating some examples as well that you are using throughout the course.

After inserting rows and creating primary keys that identify them, you learnt to look for information which is the most important and used operation on a database.

Step by step, the queries got more complicated: first, adding conditions to look for concrete rows and later, using multiple tables to obtain complex results.

And, to finish, you have learnt to delete and modify content based on search conditions.

Day 3

Congratulations!
You are now entering into the final stretch of the course.

You already know the essential things to confront simple projects
as the one you will develop in the second half of this day.
However, there are still some keywords that you need to learn
to be able to say that you know the fundamentals of SQL language.

Today is divided into two parts. In the first one you will learn
these new language functions and in the second one you will create
all the necessary queries to manage a basic blog.

Chapter 3.1
Functions

In this chapter:

1. *You will learn what a* SQL *function is.*

2. *You will aggregate rows and obtain minimums and maximums thanks to* SUM, MIN *and* MAX.

3. *You will use* CAST *to change the columns format.*

4. *You will modify texts by SQLite functions.*

What are "functions"?

SQL is a very limited language. In fact, the set of keywords that form it hardly lets us make the most basic operations.

If we need to do something more complex like aggregating the total of points of our customers or looking for the oldest tax identification number, we need a mechanism that allows us to make these searches.

To solve these problems, functions were created, new queries that let us make more sophisticated operations.

These are specific of each database and although there are some which can be considered standard, each product implements its own ones. Because of that, the first thing we must do when we start programming is to review the documents and see which are defined in the engine we have chosen.

SUM

One of the most used ones and therefore in most of the databases. Its syntax is:

Obviously, this function only makes sense when we apply it to numeric columns.

For example, to obtain the total of points, we should execute:

```
SELECT SUM (POINTS) AS TOTAL_POINTS
FROM CUSTOMERS
```

We can combine it with other operators to make more complex calculations. For example, let's calculate the average age of our customers:

```
SELECT SUM (AGE) AS AGE,
       COUNT (AGE) AS NUM_CUSTOMERS,
       (SUM (AGE) / COUNT (AGE)) AS AVER_AGE
FROM CUSTOMERS
```

AGE	NUM_CUSTOMERS	AVER_AGE
184	5	36

No, you have not made any mistake when writing the query: the result shown by SQLite is "wrong". I write it between inverted commas because for the database the result is correct, but the mistakes occur because of the type of data we are using.

If we check the structure of the table **CUSTOMERS** by the tab "Database Structure", we will see that the type of column **AGE** is INTEGER and obviously the result of the function COUNT (**AGE**) is also a full number.

Remember that in the first chapters, where the types admitted by SQLite were specified, we said that an INTEGER is a full number. So, the reason why the calculated average does not have decimal digits is that we are dividing two full numbers and, to be consistent therefore, SQLite uses INTEGER to show the result of this operation.

It is common to adapt the formats to carry out some operations, therefore all the databases include functions that allow us to convert a full number into a number with a decimal place and vice versa. In the case of SQLite, it is CAST.

CAST

To correctly calculate the average age, we need to change at least one operand in REAL, since if SQLite detects that one of the factors is a number with decimal places, the result will be with decimals.

```
SELECT
(SUM (CAST (AGE AS REAL))
/
COUNT (AGE)) AS AVER_AGE
FROM CUSTOMERS
```

AVER_AGE
36,8

MIN and MAX

They calculate the minimum and maximum of a set of values, respectively.

Let's look for the age of the youngest and oldest customers, all in the same query:

```
SELECT MIN (AGE), MAX (AGE)
FROM CUSTOMERS
```

If everything went well, the result would be 25 as minimum and 55 as maximum.

Texts handling

The three functions that we have seen up to now are under the heading "aggregate functions", it means, their objective is to obtain a result from a set of data.

Either in SQLite or the rest of databases there are many more that allows us to carry out other tasks. The ones which handle texts are the next most important.

In our table **CUSTOMERS** all the names are written in upper case so, what could we do if we need them to be in lower case? or, for example, how could we extract the letter from the **IDs** to check if it is correct?

● **UPPER** and **LOWER**: modify a text, changing it into upper or lower case respectively. Its syntax is:

 ¡IMPORTANT!

UPPER (column) / LOWER (column)

● UPPER / LOWER

● column: column whose text we want to modify.

```
SELECT LOWER (NAME) AS NAME,
       UPPER (ADDRESS) AS ADDRESS
FROM CUSTOMERS WHERE DIRECCION IS NOT NULL
```

For SQLite a capital letter is different from a small letter so it is indispensable to use these functions to look for texts. Try executing the following:

```
SELECT * FROM CUSTOMERS
WHERE NAME = 'Roberto'
```

```
SELECT * FROM CUSTOMERS
WHERE NAME = UPPER ('Roberto')
```

Since the names are stored in upper case, we will only obtain a result in the second query.

- **SUBSTR**: It allows us to "extract" a piece of a text from a string, this is the one you will have to use to identify the letter of an **ID** for example. Its syntax is:

 ¡IMPORTANT!

SUBSTR *(text, start, size)*

- SUBSTR

- *text*: text or column where we are going to apply the function.

- *start*: start position to obtain the piece of text. If it is one or more we will start counting from the left. If it is 1 or less, from the right.

- *size*: the number of letters to take from the beginning. If it is a positive number it counts to the right, if it is a negative one, it counts to the left. If we do not specify this parameter, SQLite will extract all the letters from the start position to the end of the text.

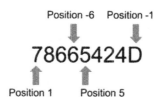

Position -6   Position -1

78665424D

Position 1   Position 5

Example of what a positive or negative position means.

Let's try all the possible options with a series of examples using the customer ID 1 (78665424D).

We start from the third position and take one character.

```
SELECT ID, SUBSTR (ID,3,1) AS EXAMPLE
FROM CUSTOMERS
WHERE MEMBER_NUM = 1
```

ID	EXAMPLE
78665424D	6

We start in the third position and do not read any letter.

```
SELECT ID, SUBSTR (ID,3,0) AS EXAMPLE
FROM CUSTOMERS
WHERE MEMBER_NUM = 1
```

We will not obtain any result.

Two letters before the one that is located in the third position.

```
SELECT ID, SUBSTR (ID,3,-2) AS EXAMPLE
FROM CUSTOMERS
WHERE MEMBER_NUM = 1
```

From the third letter to the end.

```
SELECT ID, SUBSTR (ID,3) AS EXAMPLE
FROM CUSTOMERS
WHERE MEMBER_NUM = 1
```

● **Joining texts**: The last function we are going to learn in this chapter is the one that enables us to concatenate multiple texts. For example, to show the complete name of a customer on a webpage, what we need to do is concatenate the content of the column **SURNAME** to the **NAME**.

In SQLite, there is not a specific function. We can use the operator "||" instead. For example:

```
SELECT NAME || ' ' || SURNAME AS FULL_NAME
FROM CUSTOMERS WHERE MEMBER_NUM = 1
```

FULL_NAME
ROBERTO SUÁREZ GIL

We can insert any text. For example, to show the **SURNAME**, a comma and later the **NAME**, we could execute:

```
SELECT SURNAME || ' , ' || NAME AS FULL_NAME
FROM CUSTOMERS WHERE MEMBER_NUM = 1
```

Chapter 3.2
Group by

In this chapter:

1. You will create partial groups by the keyword GROUP BY.

2. You will filter the results using the query HAVING.

Calculating subtotals

In the previous chapter we saw some functions that make operations on a set of data: SUM, MIN, MAX...

Although they are not limited in terms of the number of rows (they can be all from a table or a subset of the same), there is a limitation in the results, since we only obtain one that includes all the rows of the query.

Imagine you need to guess the number of orders done by each customer. The only way to do it would be executing a simple query SELECT for each of them, which is not practical neither viable in big databases.

In order to make these operations, SQL provides us with the keyword GROUP BY, which enables us to obtain subtotals based on a grouping criteria. Its syntax is:

 **¡IMPORTANT!**

SELECT **grouping_col_1, grouping_col_n**, function_1, function_n
[...]
GROUP BY **grouping_col_1, grouping_col_n**

- SELECT

- **grouping_col_x**: columns for whose values subtotals will be generated. For example, if the column is just the **MEMBER_NUM** of the table **ORDERS**, results for each member will be generated. On the contrary if the columns are **MEMBER_NUM** and **PRODUCT**, values for each combination of members and products will be calculated.

- function_x: any aggregate function: SUM, COUNT, MIN...

- [...]: Rest of the query including JOIN, WHERE, etc.

- GROUP BY

- **grouping_col_x**: after the keyword for grouping, we must include the same key fields of grouping as in the SELECT part.

We are going to figure out how many orders each customer has done:

```
SELECT MEMBER_NUM, COUNT (*) AS ORDERS_NUM
FROM ORDERS GROUP BY MEMBER_NUM
```

MEMBER_NUM	ORDERS_NUM
1000	3
1001	2
1002	1

Now, we are going to write a query to calculate how many times they have acquired each product and the total quantity.

```
SELECT MEMBER_NUM,
       PRODUCT,
       COUNT (*) AS TIMES,
       SUM (QUANTITY) AS UNITS
FROM ORDERS
GROUP BY MEMBER_NUM, PRODUCT
```

MEMBER_NUM	PRODUCT	TIMES	UNITS
1000	PHOTO FRAME	1	2
1000	CANDLE	2	10
1001	PHOTO FRAME	1	1
1001	CUP	1	1
1002	WALL CLOCK	1	1

We can see, for example, that the member 1000 has done two orders of candles, acquiring 10 units in total.

Selecting groups

With WHERE we can filter the rows that are taken into account in the query, whereas with HAVING we will select the subtotals to show.

It is always written after GROUP BY and its syntax is:

For example, to show those members who have done two or more orders, we can exe-
cute the following:

```
SELECT MEMBER_NUM,
       COUNT (*) AS ORDERS_COUNT
FROM ORDERS
GROUP BY MEMBER_NUM
HAVING COUNT (*) >= 2
```

MEMBER_NUM	ORDERS_COUNT
1000	3
1001	2

And to finish, we will look for products which have been bought more than once and
whose minimum purchase is the same or more than three units:

```
SELECT PRODUCT
FROM ORDERS
GROUP BY PRODUCT
HAVING COUNT (*) > 1 AND MIN (QUANTITY) >= 3
```

PRODUCT
CANDLE

Chapter 3.3
Subqueries

In this chapter:

> *1. You will create queries based on the results of other queries.*
>
> *2. You will use them to insert, modify and delete rows.*

Answering difficult questions

A subquery is a query inside another SQL query. It can be used to make complex searches or for other operations, such as, inserting the result of a SELECT query in a table.

Now, probably it is quite difficult for you to think of a situation where you would need it, but the truth is that its use is very common since we are given a lot of flexibility when making questions to the database.

For example, how could we look for all the customers who have done more orders that the **MEMBER_NUM** = 1001?

With what you have learnt up to now, the only solution is to execute two queries: in the first one you would calculate the times that customer 1001 has bought and in the second one, you would look for all the customers who have done it more times.

```
SELECT COUNT (*)
FROM ORDERS
WHERE MEMBER_NUM = 1001
```

The result is "2".

```
SELECT MEMBER_NUM, COUNT (*) AS NUM_ORDERS
FROM ORDERS
GROUP BY MEMBER_NUM
HAVING COUNT (*) > 2
```

The only customer who has gone more often to the shop (3 times, in fact) is number 1000.

By using subqueries, the query could be expressed in the following way:

```
SELECT MEMBER_NUM, COUNT (*) AS NUM_ORDERS
FROM ORDERS
GROUP BY NUM_SOCIO
HAVING COUNT (*) >
    (SELECT COUNT (*) FROM VENTAS
    WHERE NUM_SOCIO = 1001)
```

MEMBER_NUM	NUM_ORDERS
1000	3

To write a subquery, the only thing we have to do is write it between parentheses "()".

Query nesting

In the example of the subquery, an only value is generated. But, we can also work with others that give back some rows and these ones can also be used later in another query.

How could we obtain the orders of all those customers who have done more than the MEMBER_NUM = 1001?

The operations to be carried out are:

🔹 Obtaining the number of orders of member 1001:

```
SELECT COUNT (*)
FROM ORDERS
WHERE MEMBER_NUM = 1001
```

🔹 Looking for all the members who have done more:

```
SELECT MEMBER_NUM
FROM ORDERS
GROUP BY MEMBER_NUM
HAVING COUNT (*) >
    (SELECT COUNT (*) FROM ORDERS
    WHERE MEMBER_NUM = 1001)
```

🔹 Checking the orders table for those memberss:

```
SELECT * FROM ORDERS WHERE MEMBER_NUM IN
    (SELECT MEMBER_NUM
    FROM ORDERS
    GROUP BY MEMBER_NUM
    HAVING COUNT (*) >
        (SELECT COUNT (*) FROM ORDERS
        WHERE MEMBER_NUM = 1001))
```

MEMBER_NUM	DATE	PRODUCT	QUANTITY
1000	2015-01-12	CANDLE	5
1000	2105-02-14	CANDLE	5
1000	2015-06-20	PHOTO FRAME	2

Massive insertion of rows

Apart from making complex searches, we can use subqueries to insert some rows at the same time in a table of the database.

For example, imagine our physical shop goes quite well and we are going to start our online business. To manage it, we create new tables for the customers, the orders, etc. but we want all of those customers who are already registered in the shop to be also registered to buy online.

An alternative would be to create the queries INSERT based on the content of **CUSTOMER** which is only viable if the number of users is limited.

The best option is to make a query to the database and insert the result in the new one. The syntax is:

 **¡IMPORTANT!**

INSERT INTO **table_name (columns)** *subquery*

- ● INSERT INTO
- ● **table_name**: name of the table where we are going to store the data.
- ● **(column_1, column_n)**: names of the columns, separated by commas where we want to save the values. Optional.
- ● *subcquery*: SQL query whose results will be inserted in "table_name". If columns are specified, they must give back as many as indicated. If not, it must recover the same columns and types from the target table. In SQLite the subquery cannot be written between parentheses "()" (in other database engines is necessary).

We are going to store in **WEB_CUSTOMERS** all of the table **CUSTOMERS** who are not authorised for the on-line business yet:

SELECT COUNT (*) FROM **WEB_CUSTOMERS**

The result is three.

```
INSERT INTO WEB_CUSTOMERS (MEMBER_NUM, NAME, ID)
SELECT MEMBER_NUM, NAME, ID
FROM CUSTOMERS
WHERE MEMBER_NUM NOT IN
(SELECT MEMBER_NUM FROM WEB_CUSTOMERS)
```

```
SELECT COUNT (*) FROM WEB_CUSTOMERS
```

If everything went well, the result will be six.

Chapter 3.4
Views

In this chapter:

> *1. You will generate views based on* SQL *queries.*
>
> *2. You will combine them with other tables to make complex queries.*

Views as alternative to the creation of tables

A view is just a "memorised" query in the database to which we assign a name to be able to use it later as if it were any table.

Reusing queries is very useful since you do not have to write them again in full every time we want to execute them.

Its syntax is:

 **¡IMPORTANT!**

CREATE VIEW **view_name (columns)** AS *query*

- CREATE VIEW

- **view_name**: name that we will give to the view.

- **(columns)**: list of columns. It is optional and in SQLite it can only be used from version 3.9 of the database. If it not informed, it will take the names of the columns given back in the query that is generated by the view.

- AS

- *query*: query that the database will execute whenever we use the view.

We are going to create one that gives back the list of customers of the shop who are not registered in the online business:

```
CREATE VIEW PHYSICAL_CUSTOMERS AS
SELECT MEMBER_NUM, ID, NAME, SURNAME
FROM CUSTOMERS
WHERE MEMBER_NUM NOT IN
(SELECT MEMBER_NUM FROM WEB_CUSTOMERS)
```

We try to query it:

```
SELECT * FROM PHYSICAL_CUSTOMERS
```

0 Rows returned from: SELECT * FROM **PHYSICAL_CUSTOMERS**

We do not obtain any results because in the previous chapter we registered all the customers in the web table. We delete one of them to repeat the test:

```
DELETE FROM WEB_CUSTOMERS WHERE MEMBER_NUM = 1;

COMMIT;

SELECT * FROM PHYSICAL_CUSTOMERS;
```

MEMBER_NUM	ID	NAME	SURNAME
1	78665424D	ROBERTO	SUÁREZ GIL

When querying it, it behaves as if it were a table, so you can use it in combination with JOIN, UNION, functions, etc.

However, remember that a view is a memorised query so that you will not be able to modify the rows. Try executing the following:

```
INSERT INTO PHYSICAL_CUSTOMERS (MEMBER_NAME, ID, NAME, SURNAME)
VALUES (9999,'45820967Y','LUIS','CANO GORDILLO')
```

cannot modify PHYSICAL_CUSTOMERS because it is a view: INSERT INTO
PHYSICAL_CUSTOMERS (MEMBER_NUM, ID, NAME, SURNAME)
VALUES *(9999,'45820967Y','LUIS','CANO GORDILLO')*

Deleting views

The mechanism to delete views is very similar to the one of a table:

For example:

```
DROP VIEW PHYSICAL_CUSTOMERS
```

Chapter 3.5
Outer Join

In this chapter:

> *1. You will make queries similar to JOIN but obtaining not only common rows but also all the ones which are in the master table.*

Improving join operations

When we learnt to use the keyword JOIN, we saw that the database only shows the rows that fulfil the joining condition.

For example, if we run a query to obtain the name of each customer who has made orders with the acquired articles, we will see that in the list there will be only those who have bought at least once.

```
SELECT C.NAME, V.PRODUCT, SUM (V.QUANTITY) AS QUANTITY
FROM CUSTOMERS C
JOIN ORDERS V ON C.MEMBER_NUM = V.MEMBER_NUM
GROUP BY C.NAME, C.SURNAME, V.PRODUCT
```

NAME	PRODUCT	QUANTITY
JUAN	PHOTO FRAME	2
JUAN	CANDLE	10
MARÍA	PHOTO FRAME	1
MARÍA	CUP	1
ROBERTO	WALL CLOCK	1

All those customers who have never been to the shop are out of the results list.

If we need to obtain all of them, regardless if they have bought or not, we can use the LEFT OUTER JOIN whose syntax is:

 **¡IMPORTANT!**

master_table LEFT OUTER JOIN **detail_table** ON *condition*

- **master_table**: master table of the JOIN, which means, the one to which we "glue" data. All the rows will always be shown, independently whether there is coincidence in the detail_table or not.

- LEFT OUTER JOIN

- **detail_table**: table from which we will obtain the data to add to the master_table.

- ON

- *condition*: condition that two rows must fulfil in order to join. Normally, an equality of columns, which means, **column_1 = column_2**.

Let's check the results with this new type of JOIN:

```
SELECT C.NAME, V.PRODUCT, SUM (V.QUANTITY) AS QUANTITY
FROM CUSTOMERS C
LEFT OUTER JOIN ORDERS V ON C.MEMBER_NUM = V.MEMBER_NUM
GROUP BY C.NAME, C.SURNAME, V.PRODUCT
```

NAME	PRODUCT	QUANTITY
ANTONIO		
HÉCTOR		
JUAN	PHOTO FRAME	2
JUAN	CANDLE	10
LAURA		
MARÍA	PHOTO FRAME	1
MARÍA	CUP	1
ROBERTO	WALL CLOCK	1
ROBERTO		
SILVIA		

This time, we obtain a complete list of customers. The ones who are in the orders table appear with the articles they bought and the ones who are not are shown with NULL values.

As with the "normal" JOIN, we can complete the query with other keywords or functions like WHERE, GROUP BY, etc.

For example, we are going to obtain the list of customers who have bought either candles or who have not bought any article (as we have seen in the previous query, in these cases, either product and the quantity is NULL).

```
SELECT C.NAME, V.PRODUCT, SUM (V.QUANTITY) AS QUANTITY
FROM CUSTOMERS C
LEFT OUTER JOIN ORDERS V ON C.MEMBER_NUM = V.MEMBER_NUM
WHERE V.PRODUCT IS NULL
OR V.PRODUCT = 'CANDLE'
GROUP BY C.NAME, C.SURNAME, V.PRODUCT
```

NAME	PRODUCT	QUANTITY
ANTONIO		
HÉCTOR		
JUAN	CANDLE	10
LAURA		
ROBERTO		
SILVIA		

Chapter 3.6
Operations with Datetime

In this chapter:

> *1. You will learn to visualise dates in different formats.*
>
> *2. You will obtain the month, year and day of the week.*
>
> *3. You will add and subtract periods to a date.*

Manipulating dates

The type of data that was used to store dates is a specific case of SQL. You will find it almost in all databases but, it works differently in each of them. Therefore, to manipulate them, you will need to use keywords and functions which are features of the product.

For example, in SQLite and in SQL Server the type is called DATETIME whereas in Oracle it is just DATE.

To understand its functioning, the difference between the value of a DATETIME field and the format used to visualise it must be very clear:

- **Value** is the date stored and this is always "complete", which means that it contains the year, month, day, hour, minute, second and fractions of a second (in SQLite the precision is up to 1 millisecond).

- **Format** is the way the date is shown. It can be only the year (2016), a complete date in numeric format (28-03-2016) or any other that we need.

Up to now, when you wanted to obtain a datum (name, membership number, etc.) you just needed to add the name of the field in the query. In the case of the dates, as a rule, you will have to always specify the format (also called "mask") that you want to use to read it.

DATE, TIME and DATETIME

SQLite has three functions that generate the most common formats: dates (year-month-day), time (hour:minute:second) and the union of both.

We are going to use the three formats with the dates of birth that we stored in our customers table:

```
SELECT DATE (BIRTH_DATE),
    TIME (BIRTH_DATE),
    DATETIME (BIRTH_DATE)
FROM CUSTOMERS
WHERE BIRTH_DATE IS NOT NULL
```

DATE(BIRTH_DATE)	TIME(BIRTH_DATE)	DATETIME(BIRTH_DATE)
1978-08-21	00:00:00	1978-08-21 00:00:00
1979-05-03	00:00:00	1979-05-03 00:00:00
1968-06-05	00:00:00	1968-06-05 00:00:00

When we insert the data in the table, we do not specify the hour, so the field contains the value by default, which is: 00:00:00.

To check the functioning of the hours, we are going to insert a new row with the complete date in the table of orders.

```
INSERT INTO ORDERS
VALUES (1000,'2016-02-23 12:34:56','CANDLE',1);

COMMIT;

SELECT DATE (DATE), TIME (DATE)
FROM ORDERS
WHERE MEMBER_NUM = 1000;
```

DATE(DATE)	TIME(DATE)
2015-01-12	00:00:00
2015-02-14	00:00:00
2015-06-20	00:00:00
2016-02-23	12:34:56

To take into account:

- To indicate to SQLite that a datum is a date, we just need to apply the format "year-month-day hours: minutes: seconds".

- We can use only the part of the date or only the part of the time.

Fractions of a date

It is common that in certain situations, we only need to obtain a fraction of the date like the year or month. To do this, SQLite provides us with the function STRFTIME whose syntax is:

¡IMPORTANT!

STRFTIME (**format, date**)

- STRFTIME

- **format**: the format to be applied. To specify fractions of a date we must use a series of variants. In the official documentation of SQLite (*https://www.sqlite. org/lang_datefunc.html*) you can check the complete list.

- **date**: data of DATETIME type.

The most important variants of format are:

FORMAT	MEANING
%H	Hour in format 24 hours
%M	Minutes
%S	Seconds
%Y	Year
%d	Day of the month (1-31)
%m	Month (1-12)

For example, to obtain the year and month of the orders of the table that have been done any day at 12 in the morning, we could execute the following query:

```
SELECT STRFTIME ('%Y-%m', DATE) AS YEAR_MONTH
FROM ORDERS
WHERE MEMBER_NUM = 1000
AND STRFTIME ('%H', DATE) = '12'
```

YEAR_MONTH
2016-02

When the format is applied, SQLite replaces the variants %Y y %m for the parts of the associated date whereas the hyphen "-" is kept. This means a lot of flexibility when generating values from the columns which are DATETIME type.

EXERCISES

Generate dates with the following formatss:

- Day-month-year.
- Hours:minutes.
- Year minutes day.

The solution would be:

- %d-%m-%Y.
- %H:%M.
- %Y %M %d.

Modifiers

The modifiers are a type of parameter of the functions DATE, TIME, DATETIME and STRFTIME that allow us to add or subtract periods of time (hours, minutes, days, etc.) to a date. The syntax to use them is:

 ¡IMPORTANT!

STRFTIME (**format, date, modifier_1, modifier_n**)

- ◖ DATE / TIME / DATETIME / STRFTIME

- ◖ **format**: the format to be applied. To specify fractions of a date we must use a series of variants. In the official documentation of SQLite (https://www.sqlite.org/lang_datefunc.html) you can check the complete list..

- ◖ **data**: data of DATETIME type.

- **modifiers**: we can specify all that we need just by separating them with commas. They usually contain a number (the period to add or subtract) and a type (day, month, year). The complete list can be checked in: *https://www.sqlite.org/lang_datefunc.htm.*

The most important ones are:

MODIFIER	MEANING
'x hours'	Adds or subtracts hours
'x minutes'	Adds or subtracts minutes
'x seconds'	Adds or subtracts seconds
'x days'	Adds or subtracts days
'x months'	Adds or subtracts months
'x years'	Adds or subtracts years

For example, imagine that we want to survey our customers one month and 12 days after their first order. To calculate the day of the survey we could execute the following:

```
SELECT MEMBER_NUM,
     MIN (DATE) AS FIRST_ORDER,
     STRFTIME ('%Y-%m-%d', MIN (DATE), '+1 months', '+12 days')
AS SURVEY_DATE
FROM ORDERS
GROUP BY MEMBER_NUM
```

MEMBER_NUM	FIRST_ORDER	SURVEY_DATE
1000	2015-01-12	2015-02-24
1001	2015-02-18	2015-03-30
1002	2015-12-10	2016-01-22

Current date

The word *'now'* represents the current date. It acts as any other column of DATETIME type, so we can use it like that in any context. It usually goes with the modifier 'localtime' so, when it is calculated, SQLite can take into account the time zone and the possible changes summer / winter.

Try to execute the following:

```
SELECT DATETIME ('now','localtime') AS CURRENT_DATE
```

CURRENT_DATE
2016-03-30 12:46:10

"One moment, isn't there FROM?" No, and it is not necessary since as with many other products, SQLite lets us execute queries without tables as long as we only use constant values like 'now' or a determined chain of text and functions on them.

It is a very extended utility that lets us, for example, make operations like this where we just want to obtain the current date.

Chapter 3.7
Final project

Putting into practice what we have learnt

First of all, congratulations! You have reached the end of the course and so, you are ready to use SQL in the most common situations. And secondly, get ready! This little project will test you by forcing you to use all that you have learnt up to now.

For this, we are going to construct the necessary queries to manage a small blog.

The reason for choosing this type of software is that, although it may not seem so, it can be a very complex product made by lots of pieces, being the database one of the most important ones.

Think of the front page of any blog:

- In the main section, with all certainty, the posts will appear, made of texts, pictures and images that, as you can imagine, have been taken from a database.

- It is also very common to have a side navigation bar with the most visited entries, comments from the users, etc. Where is all this stored? Bingo! In the database.

- And, to finish, there will probably also be a second side navigation bar with the sections of the blog, that obviously, are also stored in the same database.

Among all the tasks to do, we have the one of designing the schema of the database that will support it and the one of preparing all the necessary queries to create and consult the posts, comments, etc.

In fact, there are many alternatives to avoid doing this "by hand" but, even so, the example is perfectly valid for the objectives that we have: putting into practice what we have learnt and see the infinite possibilities of the language.

EXERCISE 1: Definning the schema

Designing a database is not a trivial problem since we have to take into account numerous factors: which information we are going to store, how many rows the tables will have, which consults we are going to do, etc.

In this project we want to create the necessary to construct a blog so, at least, we should design tables that store:

- *Authors that can create and modify posts.*

- *Posts with the content and related information: author, date, etc.*

- *Tags that will be added to the posts to classify them.*

- *Comments created by the visitors of the blog for which it will not be necessary to be registered.*

Create a new database in SQLite (the steps are detailed in chapter 1.5) and later write the necessary queries to generate the following tables. The prefix [PK] shows that the column is part of the Primary Key of the table:

AUTHORS Table

COLUMN	TYPE	USAGE
[PK] AUTHOR_LOGIN	TEXT(30)	Login of the author.
AUTHOR_EMAIL	TEXT(100)	Email of the author.
AUTHOR_PASS	TEXT(10)	Password of the author. Usually they are stored encrypted.
REGISTER_DATE	DATETIME	Date where he or she was registered.
AUTHOR_NAME	TEXT(50)	Author name.
AUTHOR_SURNAME	TEXT(200)	Author surname.

Tabla POSTS.

COLUMN	TYPE	USAGE
[PK] POST_ID	INTEGER PRIMARY KEY AUTOINCREMENT	Unique ID of the post. The meaning of "AUTOINCREMENT" is explained in the exercises.
AUTHOR_LOGIN	TEXT(30)	Login of the person who created the post.
CREATION_DATE	DATETIME	Date when it was created.
MOD_LOGIN	TEXT(30)	Alias of the person who modified it the last time.
MOD_DATE	DATETIME	Date when it was last modified.
POST_TEXT	TEXT(5000)	Text of the post.

TAGS Table

COLUMN	TYPE	USAGE
[PK] TAG	TEXT(30)	Tag stored.
AUTHOR_LOGIN	TEXT(30)	Login of the author who used the tag for the first time.
CREATION_DATE	DATETIME	Date where the tag was created.

COMMENTS table

COLUMN	TYPE	USAGE
[PK] COMMENT_ID	INTEGER PRIMARY KEY AUTOINCREMENT	Unique ID of the comment.
POST_ID	INTEGER	Unique ID of the post in which the comment is done.
USER_LOGIN	TEXT(30)	Login of the user who comments.
USER_EMAIL	TEXT(30)	Email of the user who comments.
CREATION_DATE	DATETIME	Date when the comment was created.
COMMENT_TEXT	TEXT(1000)	Text of the comment.

*Since a comment can only belong to a post, we have added the field **POST_ID** to the table **COMMENTS**. On the other hand, columns to register modifications (user and date) have not been added to the table because it is not possible to be done in our blog.*

*The rows of the table **TAGS** are not related to the post that they refer to since it is usual that the entries of the blog share tags. This implies that we still need to create a table in the model: the one that relates the post with the tags:*

Tabla POST_TAG.

COLUMN	TYPE	USAGE
[PK] POST_ID	INTEGER	Post's unique ID.
[PK] TAG	TEXT(30)	Tag of the post.
AUTHOR_LOGIN	TEXT(30)	Author login.
CREATION_DATE	DATETIME	Date when the tag is added to the post.

Thanks to this, a post could have several tags (hence, the key is the two columns) and a tag could be added to all the entries that we want.

And with this, we can say that our model is finished.

· · · · · · · · · · · · · · · · · · · ·

EXERCISE 2: Registering authors

Very well, now that we have the skeleton of the blog (the schema of the data-base), we will define the necessary queries to manage it. We will start with the process of creation of authors.

To register a new user, we would need to:

- *Since the login of the author is PK of the table, only one user can be registered with the same alias. So, the first query to write must check if a specific alias already exists. For this, we will calculate the number of users registered with that name. If it is 0, it will mean that it does not exist.*

- *Secondly, we will store the data with INSERT.*

Obviously, we must construct the queries in a way that they are valid for any data so we will use what is called "parameters" that are just wild values in the sense that its value will be substituted by a login, name, concrete date, etc. in the moment in which the query is executed.

By convention, we are going to use the symbol ":" to identify them.

For example, to check if a login exists in the database:

```
SELECT COUNT (*) FROM AUTHORS
WHERE AUTHOR_LOGIN = ':AUTHOR'
```

And to store the data of a new user:

```
INSERT INTO AUTHORS (AUTHOR_LOGIN, AUTHOR_EMAIL, AUTHOR_
PASS, REGISTER_DATE, AUTHOR_NAME, AUTHOR_SURNAME)
VALUES (':AUTHOR_LOGIN', ':AUTHOR_EMAIL', ':AUTHOR_
PASS', ':REGISTER_DATE', 'AUTHOR_NAME', 'AUTHOR_
SURNAME')
```

• • • • • • • • • • • • • • • • • •

 EXERCISE 3: Creation of posts

At this point, you will not have problems to define an INSERT query that creates a new entry of the blog. The difficulty of this exercise consists of generating a unique identifier (POST_ID) for each of them.

We have two options:

- *Create it "by hand", which means, looking for the last post of the blog with a query SELECT MAX and later, inserting the data with the following number in POST_ID.*

- *Use an "autoincremented" field, which is a column whose value is automatically generated. It is a mechanism present in many databases, being SQLite one of the simplest ones to use since we only need to declare an INTEGER (without precision) as PRIMARY KEY AUTOINCREMENT for the database to manage it automatically.*

Let's try it with an example: execute the following query:

INSERT INTO **POSTS(AUTHOR_LOGIN, CREATION_DATE, MOD_LOGIN, MOD_DATE, POST_TEXT)**
VALUES (*'AUTHOR_LOGIN', 'CREATION_DATE', 'MOD_LOGIN', 'MOD_DATE', 'POST_TEXT'*)

*Query now the rows of the table, you will check that the entry has been created with **COD_POST** = 1.*

. . . .

 ## EXERCISE 4: Tags assignment

To fulfil this requirement, we will need three queries at least:

- *One query to check if a tag already exists in the table **TAGS**.*

- *Another one to store a new tag in that table.*

- *And, finally a query that adds a new tag for a post in particular in the table **POST_TAG**.*

. . . .

 ## EXERCISE 5: Comments creation

*Write a SQL query that adds a new row to the table **COMMENTS**. Take into account that as well as in **POST**, the PK of the table is a full "autoincremented" number.*

. . . .

EXERCISE 6: Posts modification

Let's assume that all the authors have permission to edit any post. To modify one, you will have to update the following fields for the specific entry:

- **MOD_LOGIN**: *Nick of the user who is editing it.*

- **MOD_DATE**: *Moment when it is modified. You can use the current date.*

- **POST_TEXT**: *New text of the post.*

· · · · · · · · · · · · · · · · · ·

 ## EXERCISE 7: Lasts posts

We already have all that is necessary to create the content of the blog so the next step consists in defining the necessary queries to be able to draw it on a web browser.

The first will be the one which obtains the information of the posts. Usually, on the front page on any webpage, we can only see the first 10 or 20 entries, but never the whole history. In our blog, we will only show 5, so construct a SQL that obtains the five last entries that were created.

One clue: the keywords ORDER BY and LIMIT will be very useful for you.

· · · · · · · · · · · · · · · · · ·

 ## EXERCISE 8: List of tags

To help the users browse the content of the blog, we are going to create a section on one of the sides that contains all the tags alphabetically ordered together with the number of entries that each of them have.

Design a query for it.

· · · · · · · · · · · · · · · · · ·

 ## EXERCISE 9: Entries by author

All the blogs have a section of administration only accessible to the authors and administrators. We are going to create a query that, for each author, shows the

number of posts that he or she has created, the date when he or she registered the first entry and the date when he or she published the last post.

To design it, take into account the following:

- *There is the possibility that one or some authors have not registered any entry but, even so, we want them to appear in the list, which implies that you will need to use OUTER JOIN.*

- *The number of posts and the dates of first and last publication can be generated in the same GROUP BY query with COUNT, MAX and MIN.*

• • • • • • • • • • • • • • • • • •

 ## EXERCISE 10: Related entries

And to finish, we are going to develop a very common functionality in the blogs that is showing links to related entries at the end of each post.

You can get this with a query that looks in POST_TAG for, for example, the first three entries that have some of the tags of the post which is been visualised.

Made in the USA
Coppell, TX
24 August 2021

61132201R00069